THE ARCHAEOLOGY OF THE

WESTERN MOJAVE

Gary B. Coombs

with contributions by

Richard McCarty, Tara Shepperson and Sharon Dean

Prepared by Archaeological Research, Inc. for the
United States Department of the Interior, Bureau
of Land Management under contract YA-512-CT8-160:
A Class II Cultural Resources Inventory of the
Calico, Kramer, Stoddard, Johnson-Morongo and
Twentynine Palms Planning Units, California
Desert.

Eric W. Ritter
General Editor

1979

Forward

This publication is an important work in what will hopefully be
a long and continuing series of cultural resource reports resulting
from Bureau of Land Management-sponsored studies. The Bureau is
obligated to inform the public of the results of its scientific undertakings and appears headed in the right direction.

A number of publications have previously been issued with respect
to the California Desert. These include Margaret L. Weide's Archaeo-
logical Inventory of the California Desert: A Proposed Methodology
(1973); Weide and James P. Barker's Background to Prehistory of the
Yuha Desert Region (1974); Matthew C. Hall and Barker's Background to
Prehistory of the El Paso/Red Mountain Desert Region (1975); and
Chester King and Dennis Casebier's Background to Historic and Prehistoric
Resources of the East Mojave Desert Region (1976). The Archaeology of
the Northeast Mojave Desert (1979) is a complementary report by Gary Coombs.
The response to these reports has been gratifying; most are currently
out-of-print due to public demand. Hence, these works have served as
important documents in education, and in the continuing management of and
research into the California Desert and adjoining areas.

This particular report is the outcome of diligent work by a competent
team of researchers. In establishing this contract it was necessary for
me to decide whether budget allocations were sufficient to get meaningful
archaeological survey results from an expansive area of interspersed
public and private lands. In essence, it was decided that relying on even
a very small sample, judiciously selected, was far better than depending
on fragmented, antiquated or biased data. I believe the results of this
innovative work have justified the efforts expended. Still, as amplified
in this report, the work is only a pioneering effort in furthering our
understanding of the behavior of past peoples in the western Mojave Desert.

Eric W. Ritter
General Editor

View west of Mojave River Valley near Camp
Cady Ranch, California

Rock ring in the Goldstone area, San Bernardino
County, California

CONTENTS

This report details the planning, implementation and results of a cultural resources inventory (or reconnaissance) of a 0.6% sample of approximately 1.4 million acres in the western portion of the Mojave Desert. The project was conducted in 1978-1979 by Archaeological Research, Inc. under my direction and in cooperation with the U.S. Department of the Interior, Bureau of Land Management (contract YA-512-CT8-160).

This document is intended principally as a management and research tool. It was prepared specifically for the BLM Desert Planning Staff, as an aid in the preparation of a plan, required under the Federal Land Management and Policy Act of 1976, for the protection and use of the California Desert. The report is addressed secondarily to anthropologists and historians, who may be particularly concerned with the substantive and theoretical findings stemming from the research. Non-professional readers may therefore find many of the discussions and other passages that follow to be of little personal interest. Hopefully, these readers may benefit, nevertheless, from the balance of the report.

Since this report will be accessible to a wide audience, including some who may, in using it, seek to endanger the cultural resources discussed here, I have made every effort to avoid identifying specific site locations and other sensitive information. Responsible readers will undoubtedly find these deletions somewhat of a nuisance; hopefully, they will understand my reasons for them. At present, it is planned that researchers and other qualified individuals may obtain these and related data through the BLM District Office in Riverside, California.

This report is not, nor does it incorporate, a detailed review of previous archaeological, historic and ethnographic research in the Western Mojave. Although one of its chapters is devoted to past research, this is intended only as contextual information, against which the remainder of the report may be examined and evaluated. Readers who wish to obtain more detailed information regarding the history of cultural research in the study area should consult a companion report prepared for the BLM by Environmental Research Archaeologists of Los Angeles.

The fieldwork on which the present report is based involved the reporting of _surface_ cultural materials exclusively; no excavation was undertaken. Accordingly (and also because only a handful of sites contained datable artifacts), this report does not make significant contributions to or refinements of existing desert cultural chronologies. Alternatively, I think that the report does make considerable headway toward the development of a sound, synchronic view of general post-Pleistocene settlement and subsistence patterns in the Western Mojave. These successes, in turn, are reflected in the ability of the research to meet its more fundamental objective - the differentiation of regions and zones within the study area on the basis of relative archaeological potential and cultural/historic significance.

The report contains eight chapters and a number of appendices. Chapter 1 is a general introduction, incorporating basic information regarding the study area, and the objectives and overall conduct of the research. Chapters 2 and 3 are devoted to a more specific review of the environment and cultural history, respectively, of the Western Mojave. Chapter 4 describes the Research Design Conference which gave life to the project, the procedures used in selecting the areal sample and the rationale underlying this selection.

The methods used in implementing the inventory are described in Chapter 5; included are discussions of logistical and other procedures and problems, recording techniques, daily routine and other features of the fieldwork. Chapter 6 examines several of the more important validity and reliability problems that may potentially exist in the sampling, measurement, and analysis of other aspects of the research.

The analytical results of the research are detailed in Chapter 7. The analysis focuses mainly on spatial relationships between site densities and types, on the one hand, and select environmental variables, such as landform and vegetation, on the other. Chapter 8 contains a series of recommendations, based largely upon the research, for the protection of cultural resources in the Western Mojave and for their applications in future research and education.

Two appendices accompany the published version of this report. The first contains the BLM Site Classification System and the second the BLM Desert Inventory Forms. Several additional appendices were prepared but have not been published. All of these include sensitive locational data that could easily be used to vandalize sites.

A number of people contributed, in a variety of different ways, to the research. Eric Ritter and Darrell Mahlik of the BLM provided essential technical support. Richard McCarty, Tara Shepperson, Evan Acker, Ulana Klymyshyn, Kim Geary, Sharon Dean, Cynthia Howell and Patricia Rocchio supplied the people-power necessary for the completion of the fieldwork. Consultants to the research, paid and otherwise, included Claude Warren, Margaret Lyneis, Elizabeth Warren, David Weide, Dorothy Ritenour, Gerald Smith, Dwight Read, Robert Crabtree, and several Native American consultants. Kelli Greene was responsible for all of the report typing and graphics and much of the editing and background work. Several of the above have made written contributions to this volume. Their names appear in the table of contents and at the beginnings of the appropriate chapters.

It has been a great pleasure for me to organize and coordinate this project. The California Desert is a beautiful and mysterious land. Much of its mystery derives from the many unanswered questions surrounding its cultural past. It is one thing to read of the desert and quite another to experience its nature and grandeur firsthand; but the most fulfilling step of all for me has been the attempt to solve the cultural mysteries that abound there. In this effort I have been able to share, in some very small way, the experiences of the desert peoples who have gone before. I can only hope that this research and others like it may permit a continued and growing ability to share the desert on the part of all of us.

G.C.
Santa Barbara, California
February, 1979

CHAPTER 1. GENERAL INTRODUCTION

A. Background

Under the Federal Land Policy and Management Act of 1976 (Public Law 94-579), the United States Department of the Interior, Bureau of Land Management was mandated to prepare, by October 1, 1980, a land use allocation plan for the California Desert Conservation Area. The California Desert was specifically identified in the Act because of its delicate nature from an environmental standpoint and because it is an area which is "seriously threatened by air pollution, inadequate Federal management authority, and pressures of increased use, particularly recreational use, which are certain to intensify because of the rapidly growing population of Southern California".

Among other considerations, the Act points out the need to identify, evaluate and protect the archaeological and other cultural resources lying within the California Desert Conservation Area. More generally, these same requirements are mandated under the Antiquities Act of 1906, the Reservoir Salvage Act of 1960, as amended, the National Environmental Policy Act of 1969, Executive Order 11593, and the Joint Resolution on American Indian Religious Freedom of 1978.

The Bureau of Land Management, in order to meet the October, 1980 deadline, elected to address cultural resource concerns on a regional basis and to secure independent contractors to aid in the completion of a portion of the cultural resource investigation.

The study of each Desert region would be divided further, into two parts; 1) a "Class I" Inventory, consisting of a review of existing written and other data sources, and 2) a "Class II" Inventory, consisting of an original field inventory (sample) and resulting report.

The basic objectives of the Class II Inventories are:

1. The identification and evaluation, from surface and exposed profile indications, of all cultural resource sites within a (sampled) portion of the defined area;

2. The estimation, by means of statistical analysis and other methods, of the nature and distribution of all cultural resources in the defined region;

3. The identification of the environmental and/or cultural/historical variables, or combination of variables, which may be used to predict the dispersion and diversity of cultural

resources in the defined region; and

4. The provision of a sound basis for making planning decisions concerning cultural resources in said region through field work, analysis and report preparation.

B. Project Area

On June 14, 1978, the BLM awarded Archaeological Research, Inc. a contract to conduct a Class II Inventory of five planning units located in western San Bernardino County, California: Calico, Johnson/Morongo, Kramer, Stoddard, and Twentynine Palms. This area is most easily and aptly referred to as the Western Mojave Desert region (see Figure 1-1).

The boundaries of the project area are irregular, approximately corresponding to Highway 58, the Naval Weapons Center and Camp Irwin on the north; the northern edge of Joshua Tree National Monument and the San Bernardino Mountains on the south; the San Bernardino/Los Angeles County line on the west; and the Cady Mountains, Marine Corps Training Center and the Sheep Hole Mountains on the east.

Approximately 1.4 million acres of BLM lands lie within the project domain, which also includes 1.3 million acres of private land. The contract called for an intensive survey of 0.6% of the public lands total.

C. Archaeological Research, Inc.

Archaeological Research, Inc. (ARI) is an independent, non-profit organization dedicated to the further understanding and preservation of American cultures, both past and present, through anthropological and historical research and education. Founded in 1968, ARI is the oldest anthropological corporation on the West Coast, deriving its funding from contracts, grants and private contributions.

During its history, ARI has completed research projects for the Bureau of Land Management, Bureau of Reclamation, National Park Service, Atomic Energy Commission (now the Department of Energy), Department of Health, Education and Welfare, U.S. Geological Survey, California Department of Transportation, a number of California cities and counties, and a variety of other public and private agencies.

As a non-profit organization, Archaeological Research, Inc. maintains contractual and other relationships with the University of California and the University of Nevada for the use of library and laboratory facilities, and other services. ARI is an Associate Fellow of the Santa Barbara Museum of Natural History and a member of the Santa Barbara Historical Society. Through its Directors, ARI is also affiliated with the American Association

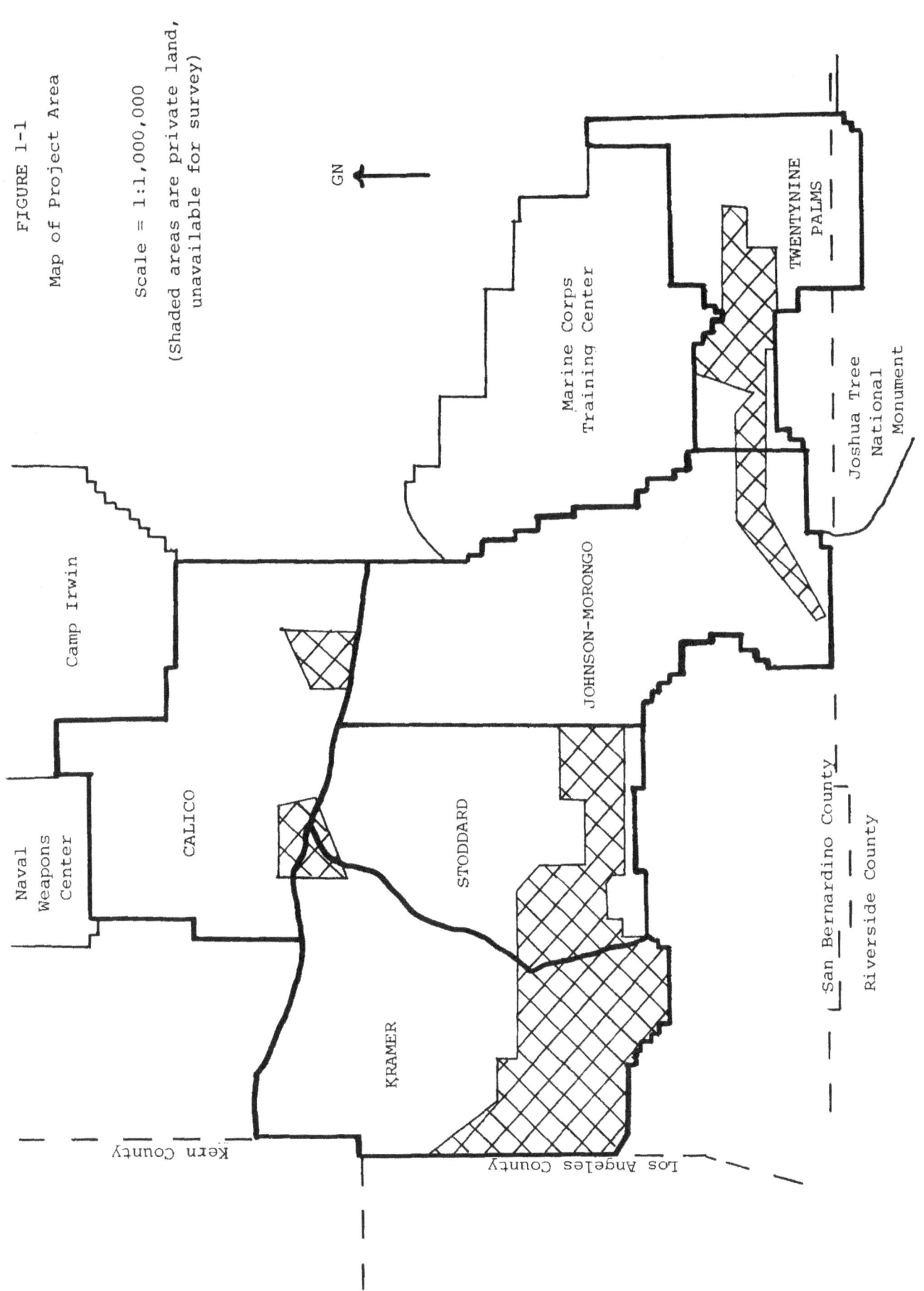

FIGURE 1-1

Map of Project Area

Scale = 1:1,000,000

(Shaded areas are private land, unavailable for survey)

GN

Camp Irwin

Naval Weapons Center

CALICO

Marine Corps Training Center

JOHNSON-MORONGO

STODDARD

KRAMER

TWENTYNINE PALMS

Joshua Tree National Monument

San Bernardino County

Riverside County

Kern County

Los Angeles County

-3-

for the Advancement of Science, American Anthropological Association, Society for American Archaeology and a number of other scientific organizations.

D. ARID-II

The project with which this report is concerned has been designated "ARID-II". This name accurately reflects the climate of the area in question, but also stands for Archaeological Research, Inc. Desert Inventory. Since ARI had previously been awarded two other contracts in the California Desert, ARID-O (a Class I Overview) and ARID-I (a Class II Inventory), the Western Mojave Project logically became ARID-II.

E. Contract Requirements

A number of specific project features were required under the ARID-II contract. These basic requirements and other guidelines were generally designed to help insure that the methods employed and the data generated by the BLM and its contractors in different desert areas would be comparable: this comparability of methods and data was considered essential to the development of an overall Desert Plan. Since the sampling design and many other aspects of this research are understandable only in terms of these requirements and guidelines, it is useful to devote some space to a brief review.

The following includes those contract specifications most directly affecting the nature of ARID-II and thus those most critical to the interpretation of the balance of this report.

1. The inventory was to consist of an intensive survey of 0.6% (8,480 acres) of the project area.

2. The survey was to involve a stratified random sample, utilizing select environmental variables (e.g. vegetation, geomorphology, water resources), considered to be meaningful in relation to prehistoric and historic activities, as sampling strata.

3. The 0.6% sample was to be divided into a minimum of 106 "sample units" or "transects".

4. Each sample unit would be 1/8 mile wide and 1 mile long, and oriented either north-south or east-west so as to conform to the existing cadastral (i.e. land ownership, or township-section) grid.

5. Sample units were to be covered on foot, utilizing four evenly-spaced sweeps (see Figure 1-2) whenever possible.

6. The classification of all archaeological sites was to be based upon the BLM Site Classification System (Appendix I).

FIGURE 1-2

Survey Path (Idealized)

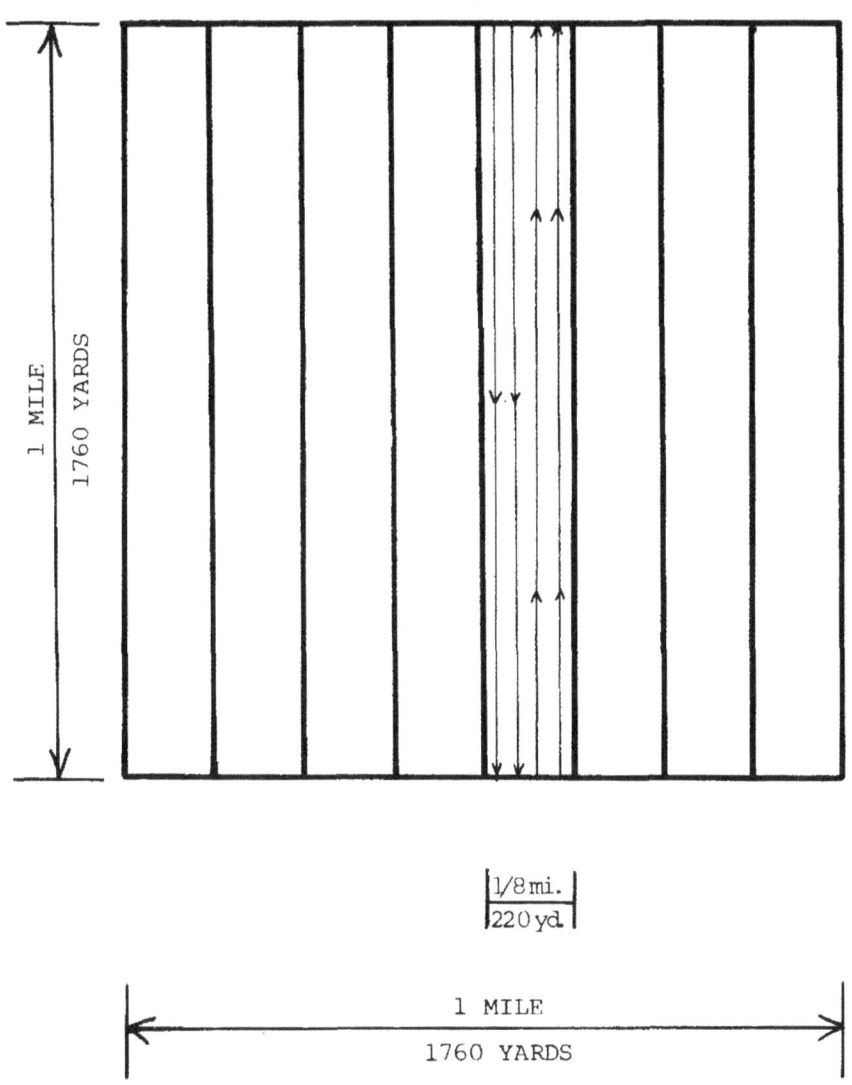

7. Site recording and the description of environmental and
    other sample unit data were to utilize existing BLM Site and
    Sample Unit Record Forms (Appendix II).

8. Site recording was to be based on surface and exposed
    profile indications exclusively; sub-surface probing was
    not permitted.

9. In general, all aspects of the research, including sampling
    design development, fieldwork, analysis and reporting, were
    to be geared to the further elucidation of archaeological
    potential, significance, and sensitivity within the project
    area.

The remainder of this report details the nature of the project
area, the methods and procedures employed in the ARID-II research,
and the results and recommendations stemming from that research.

CHAPTER 2.   ENVIRONMENTAL BACKGROUND

Richard McCarty

A.   Introduction

The Western Mojave study area (Figure 1-1) encompasses over 4000 square miles (approximately 11,000 km^2) of which 52%, or approximately 2200 square miles (5700 km^2), is under the juris- diction of the Bureau of Land Management. A number of major desert communities lie within the project area, including Barstow, Victorville, Lucerne Valley, Yucca Valley and Twentynine Palms. The Western Mojave region is defined as high desert (Bailey 1966), having generally greater valley elevations, slightly higher annual rainfall and somewhat cooler maximum temperatures than most other parts of the Mojave. The landscape is marked by scattered, iso- lated mountain areas and numerous broad, shallow dry lake basins. Elevations in the project area range from 1000 ft. (305 m.) to 7000 ft. (2135 m.) with the mode somewhere in the range of 2750 ft. (838 m.). Creosote scrub is the dominant plant community and there is a sparse population of desert-adapted animals: mostly reptiles and small rodents.

Although the Western Mojave is environmentally similar to other portions of the California Desert, there are some geomor- phological and other characteristics that set this western region apart.

B.   Landform

The dominant Western Mojave landform is known as the "Mojave Block" (Hewett 1954a), a large uplifted fault block formed by move- ment along the San Andreas Fault on the southwest and the Garlock Fault to the north. The eastern limit of the block is not clearly defined, but extends from the town of Baker to the vicinity of Amboy Crater. The entire block is tilted to the southeast so that basin elevations tend to be progressively lower as one travels in that direction. This is evident, for example, when comparing the elevations of El Mirage and Harper dry lakes (approximately 2200 ft./670 m.) with those at Dale Dry Lake and Pinto Basin (approximately 1200 ft./366 m.). Basin elevations in the remainder of the Mojave tend to be on the order of 900 to 600 ft. (275 to 183 m.).

The Western Mojave terrain does not reflect the Basin-Range pattern of deep north-south troughs and ridges that are found in the eastern portions of the Mojave. Instead, it follows the pat- tern set by the Transverse Range, with mountain areas exhibiting a characteristic northwest/southeast orientation.

This orientation is copied in a series of more or less evenly-spaced fault lines, running parallel to the San Andreas Fault and across the project area. The westernmost is the Helendale Fault, extending from the town of Helendale into the Lucerne Valley. The faults continue eastward, extending from the Black Mountain area, through the general area of Barstow, to the Twentynine Palms vicinity. The southern end of these faults terminate at the east-west trending Pinto Mountain Fault in Joshua Tree National Monument (Hewett 1954b).

C. Mountain Regions

All of the mountainous areas of the Western Mojave Desert have steep and rough terrain, characterized by slopes generally greater than 45 degrees. Upper slopes often consist of talus and areas of exposed, fractured bedrock. The predominant geologic formation of the Western Mojave's mountainous areas are Mesozoic or pre-Mesozoic quartz-bearing granites (most commonly quartz monzonite). A number of volcanic flows intrude into these granites, ranging in size from small dikes and fissures to massive exposures on the scale of the Black Mountains near Harper Dry Lake, the Malpais flow in the Rodman Mountains, and the lava buttes of the Joshua Tree and Yucca Valley area (geologic maps and texts in Dibblee 1964, 1965, 1967a; Hewett 1954a).

For the purposes of a general description, four sub-areas have been defined here that represent basic variations in the mountain topography.

1. The area outlined by the Kramer Planning Unit (Figures 1-1 and 4-3) contains some small, isolated mountains or hills, surrounded by a broad plain. These include the Shadow Mountains (4043 ft./1230 m.), the Kramer Hills (2862 ft./873 m.) and Iron Mountain (3065 ft./935 m.), as well as a number of smaller formations on the order of Red Hill. This topography is typical of the pattern found along the eastern end of the Antelope Valley, where basin elevations are near 2200 ft. (671 m.).

2. The area outlined by the Calico Planning Unit (Figures 1-1 and 4-2) and extending down to just north of Apple Valley contains a number of mountain ridges that rim several large basins and smaller valley extensions. These ridges include the Opal Mountains (3950 ft./1204 m.), the Alvord Mountains (3456 ft./1054 m.), the Calico Mountains (4542 ft./1385 m.), Stoddard Ridge (4712 ft./1436 m.), and Sidewinder Mountain (5275 ft./1607 m.). These larger ridges follow no regular pattern and are interspersed with a number of isolated hills or buttes. There is substantial variation in the basin elevations in this sub-area. For example, the elevation of Superior Dry Lake is 3009 ft. (917 m.), while that for nearby Coyote Dry Lake is 1703 ft. (519 m.).

3. A number of mountain ranges cover the east central portion of

the project area. These include the Ord (6309 ft./1923 m.),
Newberry (4829 ft./1472 m.), and Rodman mountains (6010 ft./
1832 m.). There are also several smaller mountain systems in
this region, including the Fry and Granite mountains, Iron
Ridge, and the southwestern portion of the Cady Mountains.
The Rodman and Newberry mountains together comprise the only
large block of uninterrupted mountainous territory in the
project area. They may be thought of as a northern extension
of the larger Bullion Mountains to the southeast. Their
size and elevation result in a more temperate climate than
the surrounding desert.

4. The San Bernardino Mountains are distinctive among the moun-
    tain areas in the Western Mojave because of their massive size
    and proximity to the California coast. These boundary moun-
    tains are similar, if not identical, in terms of geology, to
    the rest of the project area; yet because of differences in
    elevation, climate (cooler with more precipitation) and vege-
    tation (juniper/piñon and pine), erosional patterns and topo-
    graphy are quite different from other regions within the
    Mojave Desert.

D. Basin Regions

Most of the land in the Western Mojave consists of low pediments and shallow basins. Their surfaces are covered by recent
alluvium, or by desert pavement where the surface is protected
from sheetwash and channelling. The structure of these deposits
exhibits a well-sorted grading, from cobble-pebble alluvium on the
upper alluvial fans to fine sands on the basin floors. The playa
areas are composed of fine silts and clays and are often rimmed
with dunes of wind-blown sand.

There are fourteen defined basins within the Western Mojave
planning units and they range in size from two square miles (5.2
km^2) at Tyler Valley to over 151 square miles (391 km^2) in the
south end of Superior Valley. The average size falls somewhere
in the range of 57 square miles (148 km^2).

Basins are found throughout the project area, although the
largest number are located in Johnson and Lucerne valleys at the
base of the San Bernardino Mountains. The Johnson Valley area can
be described as a poorly-defined trough which collects runoff from
the Transverse Range and the Rodman Mountains. The large number
of dry lakes in this area is largely the result of fault action
in the base of the trough, combined with an unusually large number
of active runoff sources.

The Mojave drainage is the only river system in the project
area. It drops 1400 ft. (427 m.) as it passes through the area,
from 3000 ft. (915 m.), where it leaves the San Bernardino Mountains, at 2100 ft. (640 m.) as it passes through Barstow, to 1600
ft. (488 m.) as it leaves the study area above Afton Canyon. The

river system has created its own characteristic alluvial deposits
of river sand and gravel terraces. By its cutting action, it has
also exposed some of the earlier Pleistocene alluvium units formed
by ancient Lake Manix. These can be seen in the vicinity of Manix
Wash at the eastern edge of the project area.

E. Vegetation

Differences in geology, slope and elevation in the Western
Mojave are reflected in the various vegetation zones represented
there. In all, four major plant communities are represented:
Pinon/Juniper Woodland, Joshua Tree Woodland, and two Mojave Desert
Scrub communities, the Creosote community and the Saltbush or Alkali
Sink community (For a thorough discussion of the plants and plant
communities found in the study area, see Vasek and Thorne 1977;
Vasek and Barbour 1977; Munz and Keck 1949, Jaeger 1957).

1.   Piñon/Juniper Woodlands are confined to the southwestern
        rim of the project area in the San Bernardino Mountains. This
        community is found generally above the 4500 ft. (1372 m.) level,
        and is distinguished from other communities by the occurrence
        of Pinus monophylla, Juniperus osteosperma, J. californica,
        Quercus turbinella, and Haplopappus linearifolius.

        In the project area, there is some separation of the juni-
        per and piñon stands, resulting from somewhat distinct gradient
        and soil adaptations. Juniper prefer loose soils and shallow
        slopes, whereas piñon are usually found on steeper slopes with
        shallow soil deposits. This differentiation within the Piñon/
        Juniper zone is noticeable on a large scale by contrasting the
        members of the community found in the Juniper Flats area with
        the steep piñon-dominant slopes near Lucerne Valley and Old
        Woman Springs. The mountain regions west of Morongo Valley
        contain a mixture of juniper and piñon stands along with coastal
        varieties of manzanita (Arctostaphylos spp.) and yucca (Y.
        whipplei).

2.   The Joshua Tree Woodland community grades into the Piñon/
        Juniper zone at its upper limit and extends downward to a low
        elevation of approximately 3000 ft. (915 m.). The Joshua trees
        (Yucca brevifolia) favor gentle slopes and loose soils. These
        conditions have limited its major stands to two areas: one to
        the west and south of Victorville, easily visable on Interstate
        15 between Victorville and Cajon Pass, and a second in the
        Joshua Tree National Monument. In other parts of the San Ber-
        nardino Mountain foothills, Joshua trees are sparse and discon-
        tinuous.

        The other plant members of this community include Grayia
        spinosa, Atriplex hymenelytra, Ephedra spp., Lycium spp., and
        Salvia spp. These are found throughout the project area, along
        the upper bajadas and in some mountain areas. In other parts
        of the Mojave, this zone is occupied by blackbush (Coleogyne
        ramosissima), with or without Joshua trees.

3.   The Creosote Scrub community is by far the most extensive
in the Mojave Desert. There is an extensive list of plant
species that are often associated with the creosote bush
(Larrea tridentata); the most common associate of which
is Ambrosia dumosa. The predominance of Larrea masks
many of the subtle variations in vegetation, resulting from
differences in topography and soils, that characterize this
community.

4.   The Saltbush Scrub community is the last and, in terms of
elevation, the lowest of the major Western Mojave vegetation
zones. It is a highly specialized community, its members able
to tolerate high concentrations of salt or alkali. Some con-
stituents (e.g. Atriplex hymenelytra) are found in a variety
of desert environments. Others are limited specifically to
the moist soils of the playa beds. The Saltbush community members actually form a sucession of plant types, extending from
the basin outward and upward. Playa basins themselves are
typically devoid of any plant life. Close to the playa bor-
ders, the halophytes are encountered. The first is usually
Allenrolfea occidentalis, closely followed by Nitrophila
occidentalis, Salicornia subterminalis, Suaeda spp. and Sarco-
batus vermiculatis. At the edge of the creosote community,
Atriplex may be found.

F. Climate

The climate of the Western Mojave, like all of the Mojave
Desert, is classified as arid to semi-arid, with evaporation
greatly outstripping precipitation. Maximum summer temperatures
may reach 130 degrees F (54 degrees C), with winter lows dipping
to 0 degrees F (-18 degrees C). Average temperatures in the
project area, in January and July, are 45 and 85 degrees F (7
and 29 degrees C), respectively.

Because of the blockage of waterladen air masses by the Transverse Range and other boundary mountains, the Mojave receives very
little precipitation. Annual rates fluctuate erratically, from 15
inches (38 cm.) or more to less than one inch. The majority of
the precipitation occurs during the winter months. In the Western
Mojave, it is not uncommon for this precipitation to take the form
of snow. Any summer rains occur as short-lived thunderstorms;
while these can be severe, they are often very localized. The
Western Mojave enjoys slightly cooler maximum temperatures and
somewhat more precipitation than other parts of the Mojave at
similar elevations. This may be attributed to the area's proximity
to coastal ranges (Cooke and Warren 1973: 20).

Past climates in the project area have ranged from cool/moist
to hot/dry, and have created some significant changes in the con-
figuration of the landscape over the last 40,000 years. Evidence
of these past climates is well preserved in the old lake beds
which covered many of the basin areas in the Western Mojave,

particularly ancient Lake Manix and Lucerne Lake. On the basis of pack rat (Neotoma) middens, King (1976: 93-101) has shown that there were woodlands of piñon and juniper covering the Rodman, Newberry and Ord mountains at approximately 12,000 years B.P., and juniper woodlands covering the area up until roughly 8000 years ago.

CHAPTER 3. CULTURAL/HISTORICAL REVIEW

Richard McCarty and Tara Shepperson

This chapter represents an attempt to provide a brief review
of existing archaeological, ethnographic, and historic information
regarding past human occupation and use of the Western Mojave.
The first half of the chapter presents a historical overview of
archaeological investigations in the study area and a chronological
framework for the regional archaeology. The second half of the
chapter deals with the historic period in the Western Mojave. A
far more detailed overview of the archaeology, history and ethno-
graphy of the project area is presently being prepared for the
Bureau of Land Management by a separate contractor.

A. History of Regional Archaeology

Past archaeological interest within the Western Mojave have
had a highly selective focus. Published research has tended to
concentrate, for example, on the Mojave drainage and Pleistocene
Lake Manix, with less emphasis on such areas as Lucerne Valley,
Twentynine Palms and Morongo Valley. Moreover, while previous
investigations have provided considerable information regarding
particular localities, the majority of these have been largely
unsystematic in methods and objectives. In short, many areas
within the Western Mojave have been ignored, others have been
covered inadequately and, in general, no broadly-based, unifying
investigation has been attempted heretofore. Hopefully the present
research may be a positive step in this direction by providing data
from a widely-dispersed systematic sample covering much of the Western Mojave. As a way of initiating this unification process, let
us examine some of the major archaeological undertakings in the
study area.

1. Excavations

a. Newberry Cave - Newberry Cave was among the first excava-
    tions in the Western Mojave. The investigation involved
    several weekend projects sponsored by the San Bernardino
    County Museum (Smith et. al. 1957; Mosely and Smith 1962;
    Smith 1955 and 1963). The evidence for human occupation in
    the cave dates to approximately 4000 B.P., beginning with
    Pinto series materials (Period III). The major cultural unit
    dates to circa 1000 B.C. Other cave sites in the _____ (see
    Appendix III for this and other locational data) have also
    been recorded and some excavated (e.g. Schuiling Cave; see
    Smith 1963).

b. Calico - The Calico excavations were opened in 1964.
    Collaborators on the project have included R. Simpson,

L.S.B. Leakey, T. Clements, the San Bernardino County Museum, and the Bureau of Land Management. The excavations are in a caliche/boulder matrix dating to the mid-Pleistocene. The most recent estimate sets the date at 70,000 B.P. (Budinger 1978) with a minimum date of 45,000 B.P. (Simpson 1978). The lithic inventory includes 3000 items variously classified as choppers, knives, scrapers, bipolar flakes and modified flakes. There remains a question whether the lithics at this site were produced by man or by natural factors (Dixon 1970; Irwin 1971: 45). Other principal publications regarding the Calico Site include Leakey et. al. (1968), Schuiling (1972), San Bernardino County Museum Association (1972) and Haynes (1973).

c. SBCM-616 - This site is a salvage project begun in the summer of 1978. Some future excavations are also planned. The project was carried out by the Archaeological Research Unit, University of California at Riverside, under the direction of Carol Rector. Only a preliminary report has been prepared to date, though a published report should be available by the spring of 1979. The site is located adjacent to the Mojave River, in the _____ area. The preliminary results show the site to be generally late prehistoric. Point types indicate that the site has been occupied over the last 2000 years with a thin underlying component dated to 4330 ± 100 at the U.C. Riverside ^{14}C Lab.

d. Lucerne Valley - Two unreported excavations by C. Becker and P. Wilke have been conducted in Lucerne Valley (Gerald Smith, personal communication). Information regarding these should be available soon. T.J. King (1976) has published a report on the Lucerne Valley area in which he synthesizes information from many of the available collections.

2. Surveys

a. Black Canyon - Black Canyon has generated a great deal of interest because of petroglyphs found in the canyon (Smith et. al. 1961; Turner, Popiano and Reynolds 1971; Smith and Turner 1977; Turner 1978; and Mosely and Smith 1962). Investigations by Wilson Turner in Black Canyon are continuing at this time. L. Hidy (1971) has surveyed portions of the Harper Dry Lake region, just south of Black Canyon.

b. Manix Basin/Calico Mountains Region - R.D. Simpson has conducted a number of surveys in the Manix Basin and the general area of the Calico Mountains. These have been related to her work in locating Early Man sites in the Mojave. The published reports have focused on an area known as Coyote Gulch (Simpson 1961), the eastern Calico Mountains (Simpson 1960) and the Lake Manix vicinity (Simpson 1958, 1964, 1965, and 1969).

c. Mojave River - G.A. Smith and others associated with the

San Bernardino County Museum have conducted a walking tour
of both sides of the Mojave River and in the Manix Basin
area (Smith et al. 1957; Smith 1963 and personal communication).

d. Lucerne Valley/Twentynine Palms - The area around Twentynine Palms was surveyed extensively during the 1930's
(Campbell 1931; Campbell and Campbell 1935). Archaeological site reports from the Lucerne Valley area have been
analyzed by T.J. King (1976).

Although this review of excavations and surveys does not exhaust
the list of available information on the project area, it does reflect the general foci of archaeological attention within the region,
indicating, among other trends, that many comparatively large tracts
of land are not covered in any existing reports.

B. Chronological Framework for the Regional Archaeology

There has not been a prehistoric chronology established that
applies specifically to the Western Mojave, nor one that covers
all temporal periods of occupation. There are, however, several
general chronologies dealing with the last 10,000 years in the
Mojave Desert that are applicable (Warren and Crabtree, in press;
Hester 1973; Wallace 1962 and 1978; King 1976). These are based
primarily on the ordering of point types, supported by ^{14}C dates
and other data.

The results of excavations and surveys in the project area
concur with the general framework identified for the California
Desert, even though the Western Mojave has been influenced by the
people of the San Bernardino Mountains and adjoining coastal regions.
Also, the Calico site may significantly extend the time span of human
occupation in the project area. Because of the uniqueness of Calico
and the speculative nature of the data (and to avoid any confusion
that may result from period numbering systems applied by previous
writers), the Pleistocene will be considered apart from the other
periods.

1. Late Pleistocene Period (70,000 to 20,000 B.P.)

More attention has been paid to the Late Pleistocene than
to any other period represented in the Western Mojave. Nevertheless, because of the controversies that surround the finds
at Calico and the interpretations of the materials from Coyote
Gulch (Simpson 1961) and Manix Basin (Simpson 1964), the period
must still be considered highly problematical.

Calico stands virtually alone as possible evidence for
Pleistocene human occupation in the Americas (cf. Bryan 1978).
Arguments over whether the "tools" discovered there are artifacts or geofacts (Haynes 1973) still persist. The environmental setting of the site has also been a problem. In spite

of the labor and expense dedicated to the site, it will take more convincing data and results before most archaeologists are willing to state that human occupations of the Western Mojave extends into the Pleistocene.

Cultural materials alleged to be from the later part of this Period, from 40,000 to 20,000 B.P., have been named, collectively, the Manix Lake Lithic Industry in the northern portion of the study area. In general discussions, the name Malpais Complex has been applied. "Malpais", a term coined by Malcolm Rogers (1939: 6-23), refers to the pre-projectile point industries found throughout the California Desert. The artifacts consist of large bifaces or blanks, choppers, cores and flakes. The pattern of flaking shows numerous step fractures and deep bulbs of percussion, indicating a crude, hard-hammer technique of manufacture. While the sites are probably older than 10,000 years, their true antiquity is difficult to substantiate, since most of the sites occur on desert pavement and could have been deposited any time after the formation of the pavement. The lack of points and the simple technology argue for an early date, yet as Glennan (1976) points out, the materials could be merely the refuse from lithic workshops. The occurrence of these sites in the vicinity of natural lithic deposits in the Manix Basin supports Glennan's argument. More work and new methods are the best hope for fitting this tool assemblage into its proper time frame.

2. "Period I" (10,000 to 5,000 B.C.)

A number of terms have been used when discussing this Period: Lake Mojave, San Dieguito, Haskomat, Fallon Phase, Western Lithic Co-Tradition, and Western Pluvial Lakes Tradition. Among these, two terms - San Dieguito and Haskomat - present a well-defined interpretation of the lithic assemblages and general economy of the early inhabitants of the Western Mojave.

The San Dieguito Complex, as defined by Warren (1967), combines Rogers' San Dieguito (I through III) and Playa complexes and the Lake Mojave lithics. San Dieguito has been interpreted as a generalized hunting tradition that was widespread in the California Desert and in the Western Great Basin. The sites are generally found in association with river and lakeshore environments; and inhabitants enjoyed a cooler and moister climate than is found in the Mojave today.

The lithic assemblage includes leaf-shaped or ovate points, knives, graving tools, a variety of domed scrapers, and crescents. The manufacturing technique is crude, producing irregular edges and some deep bulbs of percussion. Many of the characteristics of San Dieguito are similar to those of the Malpais Complex discussed above. A major distinction is the extended inventory of artifacts in the former, including the Lake Mojave point series found in association with other San Dieguito materials at several site locations. The most noted of these locations is the Harris Site in San Diego County (Warren and True 1961), generally considered the type site for San Dieguito. The dates for the assemblage at the Harris Site range from 7080 to 6000 B.C.

The Haskomat Complex (Warren and Ranere 1968) is also comprised of a number of different assemblages. Haskomat sites are even more dispersed than San Dieguito, encompassing the Mojave Desert, and the Western and Northern Great Basin. Materials from the Haskomat and San Dieguito complexes overlap stylistically in some ways, and Lake Mojave points are included in both. Nevertheless, the tool types and manufacturing techniques are generally different; Haskomat artifacts, for example, reflect more refined thinning and pressure flaking. The characteristic point type for Haskomat is similar to the "Haskett" point, with long sloping shoulders and a long, parallel-sided stem. Other artifacts include a number of unusually shaped scrapers as well as spoke shaves, gravers and crescents. The assemblage is usually assigned a time span of 8000 to 5000 B.C.

At Lake Mojave, fifty miles (80.5 km.) west of the study area, both San Dieguito and Haskomat materials have been reported. Lake Mojave points have also been recorded at various locations within the study area (King 1976; also, the present report). King also illustrates two other lanceolate points - a Lind Coulee and a Black Rock Concave - assigned to this period, which were collected from Lucerne Valley.

3.   "Period II" (5000 to 2000 B.C.)

This time span is one of the poorest known in the Mojave Desert chronology. The problems come from the sites representing this period, the point types used as time markers and the environmental and related economic factors shaping this period.

The two type sites for Period II are the Pinto Basin Site (Campbell and Campbell 1937) and the Stahl Site (Harrington 1957). The fact that the Pinto Basin Site is represented by surface remains severely limits our ability to resolve many of the thorny questions relating to the sequences and dating of point types and their relation to the environment. Results from the Stahl Site suffer from an unsophisticated set of questions asked in the field at the time of excavation - a comment on the state of the art at the time, not on the skill of the excavators.

Point types represented here include the Silver Lake series, the Humboldt series, and the Pinto series. All three types have been reported in the Mojave and at various locations in the Great Basin.

The Silver Lake point type (or types) is similar in form to Lake Mojave points. The two types are found in association

at Lake Mojave and at other locations (Campbell et al. 1937:
84; Harrington 1957). The Silver Lake series seems to have
outlasted the Lake Mojave type and is found at the Pinto Basin
Site and the Stahl Site. No dates have bee assigned to this
type, although it is believed to extend from Period I to
approximately 4000 B.C.

The Humboldt series has been dated at a number of sites
in the northern Great Basin. Numerous finds have been reported
in the Mojave as well, although no dates have been obtained.
The general form of the points is lanceolate to triangular,
and they are comparatively large. The variants include two
concave base types and a basal notched variety.

The Pinto series is the best known of the three types but
is also the most confusing. Five variants were originally
defined by Harrington (1957). Later attempts to remedy some
of the problems (including renaming the series "Little Lake"
[Lanning 1963]) have only created more terminology and more
confusion. The form of the points is generally triangular
with weak shoulder attributes (the basis for the types) and
a shallow concave base. Dating of the Pinto series falls
between 3350 and 670 B.C. (Hester 1973). Besides the Silver
Lake-Humboldt-Pinto series of point types, the artifact inventory for this period includes a number of types of scrapers
and scraper planes, as well as drills, gravers and milling
stones (cf. Harrington 1957).

The lack of substantiating data regarding this period
has led to a number of arguments. Some authors (cf. Hester
1973; Wallace 1962) take the position that there was a hiatus
in the California Desert during the Altithermal, roughly 6000
to 4000 B.C. According to this argument, the people who returned
at the end of the Altithermal had an economy based on hunting
and collecting, somewhat different from the generalized hunting
tradition of the previous period. Others (Susia 1964; Warren
and Crabtree, in press) believe that the close resemblance of
artifact assemblages between Periods I and II suggests a continuation of tool types and occupation through the Altithermal and
a persistence of the economic emphasis on hunting, rather than
on food collecting (cf. Wallace 1978; 28). Until more carefully collected information on artifact assemblages is available, as well as information on the magnitude of the Altithermal
in the Mojave, the question of the hiatus and a changing economy
will remain unanswered.

4. "Period III" (2000 B.C. to A.D. 500)

This Period contains a number of well-defined point types
(Elko series, Gypsum Cave, Humboldt Concave Base), some of which
have been used successfully as fairly precise time markers in
the Great Basin (O'Connell 1967) and the Mojave Desert (Lanning
1963). A number of labels have also been attached to this

Period. The most common are Amargosa I (Rogers 1939), the
Newberry Period (Bettinger, O'Connell and Taylor 1972), and
the Early and Middle Rose Springs phases (Lanning 1963; Clewlow,
Heizer and Berger 1970).

The size of the points has been a critical factor in the
interpretation of the period; all show a trend toward a medium
to large size with a variety of notching and stem types. At
Newberry Cave, these points have been found in association with
dart shafts linking their use to the pre-bow and arrow period
of the atlatl.

The greater number of grinding implements found during
this period suggests increased attention to plant processing
as an addition to the previous hunting economy. The discovery
of split twig figurines indicates that there were some influences from the Southwest at this time. G.A. Smith reports
uncovering a number of items, including split-twig figurines,
that appear to be related to hunting magic involving bighorn
sheep, dating to 1020 B.C. (Smith et al. 1957; Smith 1963;
Hubbs, Bien and Suess 1965: 111). Somewhat similar finds have
been reported at a slightly earlier date from the Grand Canyon
region (Euler 1967; Schwartz, Lange and DeSaussure 1958), suggesting a westward diffusion of the trait.

Towards the end of this period, there are indications of
increased contact with the Southwest. Occurrences of Southwestern pottery are reported from several locations in the
Mojave. There is also evidence for the introduction of the
bow and arrow as small point types of the same general form
begin to replace the larger dart point varieties.

5.   "Period IV" (A.D. 500 to 1000)

In the Western Mojave area, this period is essentially an
extension of Period III, with the addition of smaller points
brought about by the introduction of the bow and arrow. The
most common point types of this time are the Middle and Late
Rose Springs series (Lanning 1963). The Cottonwood point
type appears by the end of Period IV.

There are some indications that the Western Mojave, like
many other locations in the Mojave, was being used by the
Anasazi as a trade route to the Pacific, and for the region's
turquoise resources. Most of this activity was carried out in
the eastern sections of the Mojave near Halloran Springs, although there are some reports (Smith and Leonard, personal
communication) of turquoise mining along the Mojave River west
of Barstow, associated with typical Anasazi black-on-gray pottery. These sites, however, probably represent a very sporadic
occupation.

6. "Period V" (A.D. 1000 to Ethnographic Present)

Abandonment of the permanent Anasazi settlements in the southern parts of Nevada and Utah at the beginning of this period ended their influence in the Mojave. At this time, there is a noticeable change in point types, as the Cottonwood series and the small Desert Side Notched series become the predominant types. These points are generally associated with the Numic expansion throughout much of California and the Great Basin.

A few occurrences of Colorado River pottery types in the Western Mojave attest to influences from these Hakataya groups. Hakataya occupations have been reported in the Cronese Basin, just east of the study area. From ethnographic accounts, there is evidence of other movements of these Colorado River peoples. It is reported that during the 17th and 18th centuries, the central portion of the Mojave was abandoned by the Mohave Indians and the area was occupied by the Chemehuevi. More recent occupations are discussed in the following section.

C. The Historic Period

The establishment in 1769 of the first Spanish mission, San Diego de Alcala, stimulated the exploration and charting of Southern California. Nonetheless, by 1776, the Anza route between the California coastal missions and the Arizona and Sonora regions was scarcely known because of the severe desert crossing. Although this route was situated far south of the study area, its discontinued use after the Yuma Indian insurrection of 1781 led to an extensive search for a more northerly route.

At the time of European intrusion, the Western Mojave was largely occupied by two aboriginal groups, the Serrano and Vanyume. The Serrano occupied territory east of Cajon Pass in the San Bernardino Mountains, as far as Twentynine Palms, including the Victorville region, and as far south as Yucaipa Valley, outside the study area. The Vanyume were a sparse, poor population that lived along the Mojave River. While the Vanyume language is unknown, they were likely members of the Serrano language family (Bean and Smith 1978: 570).

In 1776, Francisco Garcés pioneered a route through the Mojave Desert. Guided by Mohave Indians, Garcés traveled an ancient trail from the Mohave villages at the Colorado River to Soda Springs (south of Soda Lake), then up the Mojave River. Garcés crossed the river near a point later named "Forks in the Road", near the present town of Yermo. Garcés travelled generally up the Mojave River drainage to the foothills of the San Gabriel and San Bernardino Mountains (Hafen 1954: 73-81); he had completely traversed the Western Mojave before reaching the San Gabriel Mission.

Garcés journeyed into the San Joaquin Valley before returning to the mission at San Gabriel. His route across the Mojave Desert varied slightly from the first trail, but Garcés return to the Mohave villages demonstrated that a northern route was possible across the California Desert. However, although an alternative to the Sonora route had been found, the significance of the Mojave Trail went unrealized for many decades. Garcés was killed in the 1781 Yuma uprising, and in the next forty years few non-Indians crossed the Western Mojave. The only exceptions documented are travelers along the eastern Sierra Nevada foothill trail between Cajon Pass and Oak Creek (Warren and Roske 1978).

Father Francisco Garces called all the Serrano and Vanyume peoples he met by the name "Beneme" - his interpretation of the Mohave Indian name for these people. His accounts are among the earliest descriptions of the Vanyume and Serrano. On two separate occasions during his trek along the Mojave River, Garcés was cordially greeted by the "Beneme". Of one instance he writes: "In this rancheria, they regaled me with hares, rabbits, and great abundance of acorn porridge, where with we relieved the great neediness we had" (Hafen 1954: 77).

The missionization process disrupted the social organization of both of these groups. The Vanyume were absorbed rather quickly by missions or assistencias and, as an ethnic group, were extinct before 1900. While the Serrano living near the coast and in the San Bernardino Mountains were moved bodily to the missions, the northeastern Serrano maintained some autonomy. Today, Serrano people are found mainly on the Morongo and the San Manuel reservations.

The Western Mojave region was crossed again by the Spanish in 1819. Leading a punitive expedition of about fifty men, Gabriel Moraga followed the Mojave Trail eastward in pursuit of fleeing Mohave Indians. The party followed the Mojave River through the study area into the desert around Kelso, where they ran short of supplies. Although the party had been able to follow the trail along the river, once in the open desert, Moraga became lost and turned back (King and Casebier 1976: 284).

Between 1827 and 1831, several expeditions from the east crossed the California Desert, and trade and travel routes were established. Jedediah Smith (1826 and 1827), Ewing Yount (1829), and the Wolfskill-Yount party (1830-31) all followed the Mojave Trail across the desert, through the Western Mojave and into the San Bernardino Mountains. Antonio Armijo (1829-30) entered California farther north, forging a trail that veered south and met the Mojave River near the study area. Between 1830 and 1848, these alternate routes became major lines of communication between Alta California and New Mexico.

In 1829-30, Antonio Armijo journeyed from New Mexico in search of a commercial trade route to California. While it has traditionally been accepted that Armijo's route entered California near

Pahrump Valley, finally meeting the Mojave River in the Barstow area, recent research by Elizabeth von Till Warren suggests that later caravans entered further south, near Paiute Valley, linking up with the Mojave Trail east of the study area (Warren 1974: 79-81).

It seems likely that the more southerly route proposed by Warren became the Old Spanish Trail, although some other alternate routes were probably limitedly used. Armijo's route near Death Valley via the Amargosa River was known, although it was little used until the 1850's when it became the Salt Lake-Los Angeles Wagon Road. It joined the Mojave Road at Forks in the Road (Yermo).

Until 1848, the bulk of activity along the Old Spanish Trail consisted of the official caravans between Santa Fe and Los Angeles. Each fall, Mexican traders packed woolen goods, especially blankets and other manufactured items, to exchange for horses. Then, the next spring the traders would herd the horses and mules to New Mexico. The large herds dessicated the landscape along the trail. John Charles Fremont, in his 1844 travels across the Mojave Trail, noted the destruction caused by the horse and mule caravans:

> ...the annual Santa Fe caravans, which luckily
> for us had not made their yearly passage. A
> drove of several thousand horses and mules would
> entirely have swept away the scanty grass at the
> watering places...(Hafen 1954: 288)

Captain Fremont traveled much of the Mojave/Spanish Trail in 1844. Heading east from the coast, he followed the trail from Oak Creek to a site near Oro Grande and downstream below Forks in the Road. Some of his narrative has interesting descriptions of the Mojave River, which he appropriately named the "Inconstant River".

> A clear bold stream, 60 feet wide and several
> feet deep, had a strange appearance running
> between perfectly naked banks of sand. The
> eye, however, is somewhat relieved by willows,
> and the beautiful green of the sweet cotton-
> woods with which it is well wooded, as we
> follow along its course, the river, instead
> of growing constantly larger, gradually
> dwindles away, as it was absorbed by the
> sand (Hafen 1954: 287-8)

With the end of the Mexican War in 1847, Americans began to establish homes in California. Emigrants and survey crews appeared in the Western Mojave, and soon military camps, trading posts, and settlements were underway. In 1851, the short-lived Chorpenning mail service carried mail between San Francisco and Salt Lake via Los Angeles and the Mormon Road, which followed the Mojave River through the study area. Among the first Anglos to arrive in the study area were surveyors for the railroad.

The 1850's was a decade of great controversy. Following the
1849 Gold Rush, the population of California grew rapidly and
there was increasing demand for a railroad to connect with the
East. In 1853, Congress authorized a series of railroad surveys a-
long various proposed routes. The 35th Parallel route, aligning
Los Angeles with Albuquerque, stimulated a number of surveys along
the route through the Western Mojave.

The first railroad explorer of the Mojave Desert was a civilian
trader, Francois X. Aubry. After driving a flock of sheep to California in 1852-3, along the Yuma Trail, Aubry returned to New Mexico
along the 35th Parallel route. While the exact route of Aubry is
not known, he is sure to have entered the Western Mojave and followed
the Mojave River for several days. In 1854, Aubry made another
round-trip, passing through the Western Mojave again that summer
(Chaput 1975: 110-124).

Between Aubry's visits to the area, the Western Mojave was explored by two army engineers. Lieutenant Robert S. Willimson followed the Mojave River to is sink, and at last discredited the
notion that the Mojave River fed into the Colorado. Lieutenant
Amiel W. Whipple led a large party along the Mojave Trail (King
and Casebier 1976: 290).

Numerous other surveys were undertaken, directed by the State
of California. The United States Government laid out township
grids in the Western Mojave. Few of these surveys have added
lasting knowledge of the area, since in many cases stakes and
markers could not be relocated (Edwards 1959).

While the interest in a railroad continued, attention was
focused also on wagon roads and postal routes. There was no good
stage route to the east, and mail was still being sent around Cape
Horn (Chaput 1975: 15).

From 1857 to 1861, survey and road improvement work along the
Mojave Trail was conducted by Edward Fitzgerald Beales. Although
Beales' instructions did not include work in California, Beales'
men improved the trails. This work was sensationalized by his use
of camels as pack animals (King and Casebier 1976: 291-2).

Beales' work on the 35th Parallel attracted nation-wide attention. By 1858, emigrant wagon trains were using his road, and a
second mail service commenced October 1, 1858. The growing opti-
mism and increased use of the road soon evaporated with an Indian
attack on a wagon train (Casebier 1975). Consequent punitive
action against the Indians resulted in the establishment of military outposts in the Western Mojave.

In April, 1859, Major William Hoffman led a large military
party to the needles of the Colorado River, near the site of the
Mohave villages. Here, with a show of strength, he established
a military post named "Fort Mojave". The establishment of Fort

Mojave created a need for the shipment of supplies across the Desert and increased military action along the Mojave Road (Casebier 1975: 77-94).

In April, 1859, Captain James H. Carleton was sent to punish Paiutes presumed guilty of depredations along the Mojave Trail. He established a base camp about ten miles east of Forks in the Road which he named "Camp Cady". Although the camp was soon abandoned, it was re-used occasionally by patrols of the California Volunteers. On April 23, 1865, Camp Cady was regarrisoned, first by volunteers, then by regular army, until 1871 (Casebier 1972: 5-8).

On July 29th, 1866, the Camp Cady "incident" occurred. While there is no need to detail the skirmish here (see Casebier's [1972] complete description), the blundering attack on a group of Indians shows the soldiers' fear of the Paiutes, and helps explain why the outpost was garrisoned for a number of years.

As Indian conflicts came to an end, the Western Mojave became a focal point of civilian growth. Emigrants passed through the area along either the Salt Lake Road or the Mojave Road (by then known as the Government Road). Mining developed, attracting people to the area in increasing numbers. Several trading posts were established along the routes of travel, some growing into small settlements. Major suppliers were Lane's (Oro Grande), Grapevine (near Barstow), Fish Pond (Nebo) and Hawley's in Yermo (Norris and Carrico 1978: 38).

While the big mining booms in the region did not occur until the 1880's, lesser strikes took place between 1865 and 1875 near Stoddard Wells (Helendale), the Picacho and Oro Grande areas, and near present-day Twentynine Palms (Norris and Carrico 1978: 44). The Ivanpah boom of the 1870's stimulated travel through the region, but no permanent settlement resulted. It was not until the big discoveries of the 1880's that there was a major influx of people to the Western Mojave.

In 1880, the first big silver strike occurred at Waterman, near the present site of Barstow. The Waterman mine was owned by Robert Whitney Waterman and John L. Porter. To process the silver bullion, a mill was set up along the banks of the Mojave River. Around this 10-stamp mill, the Waterman townsite developed. It was character- ized by bunk houses and boarding houses, although the town also had a few homes, a store, a post office, an assay office, and a school. In just one year, Waterman became the largest city between San Bernardino and the Colorado River. Between 1880 and 1887, 70,000 tons of ore were extracted, valued at $1,700,000 (Belden 1952).

Twenty miles east of Twentynine Palms, the Dale Mining District was established early in the 1880's. Claims were originally filed on the Supply and Virginia Dale mines. Nearby grew up the town of

Dale, and a stamp mill was established. In the 1880's, residents
moved six miles south to a small valley and established the town
of New Dale (Belden 1954). The Dale Mining District remained in
continuous operation until World War I and was sporadically active
after that at such mines as the Gold Crown and the Brooklyn. Some
limited mining activity is still carried out in the area.

Another silver discovery in the Calico Mountains created another
overnight boom town of more than 1000 persons. The Silver King
Mine proved very productive, and the nearby town of Calico had the
rough and ready character of a mining camp, although it did support
a weekly newspaper, Calico Print, from 1882 to 1887 (Belden 1952).

There were several other important silver and gold mines in
the Western Mojave. The Waterloo Mine, two miles west of Calico,
was owned by the Oro Grande Mining Company. Silver was hauled
forty miles to the stamp mills at Oro Grande (Zeitelhack and La
Barge 1976: 96-104). Coolgardie, Copper City and Goldstone
communities blossomed near productive placer mines (Payne 1976:
108).

Continued growth of desert mining activity was coupled with
the arrival of the long awaited railroads. Not only were lines
opened connecting with the east, but small feeder railroads were
built, allowing more efficient hauling of ore. Railroads also
stimulated several new towns at stations along the line.

In 1882, the Atchison, Topeka, and Santa Fe Railroad began
laying track eastward from Mojave toward Needles. It became most
active after 1885, when the Waterman Junction (Barstow) to Los
Angeles track was completed. In 1903, construction of a railroad
line began from Daggett along the new San Pedro, Los Angeles and
Salt Lake railroad route. This line became known as the Union
Pacific in 1921 (Myrick 1963: 623-647, 765-766).

The Western Mojave continued to develop. Homesteaders moved
to the lower Mojave River Valley; dry farming was undertaken in
Lucerne Valley and Apple Valley, and new mining and quarrying
activities began. After the turn of the century, gold mining was
concentrated at the continually active Dale mines, the Orange
Blossom Mine (which had a short career in 1907), and the Bagdad
Chase mines near which the town of Stedman was established. The
Goldstone-Goldbridge area boomed again in the early 1920's (Norris
and Carrico 1978: 60-62). These mines were now corporate operations.

Borax, an important product of the Northeastern Mojave Desert,
also became a commercial commodity in the Western Mojave at Marion.
The Pacific Coast Borax Company built a crushing and drying plant
for ore extracted from the eastern Calico Mountains (Zeitelhack
and La Barge 1976: 100-101).

The cement industry developed into a major activity within the
Western Mojave. The Golden State Portland Cement Company was

situated in Oro Grande and remains today under the name of the Riverside Cement Company. The Southwest Portland Cement Company established a plant at Leon, along the Mojave River, and spawned the town of Victorville one mile to the south (Myrick 1963: 857-858).

Corporate mining and quarrying led to construction of a number of small railroad lines for the more efficient hauling of ore. Some examples are the Bagdad -Chase railroad spur, the Mojave Northern railroad, and the Pacific Coast Borax line which ran from the crushing and drying plant at Marion (between Calico and Daggett) and the colemanite beds in the Calico Mountains (Zeitelhack and La Barge 1976: 100-101). While most of these railroad lines were used only for industrial purposes, the Northern Mojave Railroad provided passenger service from 1915 to 1925 (Myrick 1963: 861).

Other small railroad lines in the study area include the San Bernardino Mountain Railroad which runs from Victor Valley eastward. The Adelanto Spur runs northwest from Leon, and now serves George Air Force Base. In 1955, the Permanente Cement Company developed the Lucerne Valley Branch of the Santa Fe between Hesperia and Cushenberry (Myrick 1963: 864-865).

The arrival of the railroad to some extent altered wagon travel routes. Major roads crossing the desert became aligned with the railroad tracks, since a secure supply of water was available at the frequent railroad maintenance and way stations (for a detailed account of routes in the California Desert, 1776-1880, see Warren and Roske 1978). In the first two decades of the 20th century, many automobile routes were established within the Western Mojave. Many of these are detailed in U.S. Geological Survey Water-Supply Papers #224 and #490-B (Mendenhall 1909; Thompson 1921).

Beginning in the 1920's, the Western Mojave was traversed by car. Travelers now were often seeking recreation. Victorville and Twentynine Palms were two resort areas which were foci of vacationers. Victorville maintained an image of a real "Western Town", featuring guest ranches, saloons, and rodeos (Norris and Carrico 1978: 78-79). The Desert became more accessible in the 1930's when two major east-west highways were paved, U.S. 66 (now supplanted by Interstate 40) and U.S. 91 (parallelling Interstate 15).

With the advent of World War II, the military took control of much of the California Desert. While General Patton's Desert Training Program was concentrated further east, several military bases were established within the Western Mojave In 1940, a large tract of land northeast of Barstow was set aside for Camp Irwin. Near Twentynine Palms, a glider training base was set up in 1941. Both of these sites were also utilized as armored division training areas. Army Air bases were established near Daggett and Victorville, and supply depots were placed at Nebo and Yermo. These were taken over by the Marine Corps after World War II (Norris and Carrico 1978: 97-99).

At the time of the Korean Conflict in the early 1950's, military bases were reactivated. In 1952, a large Marine Corps Training Center was established at Twentynine Palms. These bases continue in operation today (Norris and Carrico 1978: 116).

Since World War II, the Western Mojave has been experiencing a boom in urban growth. Much of this expansion centers around Victorville, Hesperia and Apple Valley, and near Twentynine Palms and Yucca Valley. Along with an increased number of year-round occupants, and persons with week-end homes, there is an ever growing number of visitors to natural areas such as Joshua Tree National Monument, established in 1936. Off-road vehicle users, rockhounds and relic hunters have significantly stepped up their activities in the area.

Accessibility to the study area was made easier by the establishment of an interstate freeway system. The interstates have caused considerable alteration of traffic routes, often leading to the closing of service-oriented towns along the older roads. At the same time, the high desert has become a destination for week-end travelers from the Los Angeles metropolitan area.

CHAPTER 4. RESEARCH AND SAMPLING DESIGN

Gary Coombs and Richard McCarty

On July 1 and 2, 1978, Archaeological Research, Inc. conducted
a conference on the campus of the University of Nevada, Las Vegas,
for the purpose of developing a research design for the ARID-II
fieldwork. The sampling design which is outlined in the following
section, was a direct result of this conference. Following a detailed look at the sampling design itself, we will describe the
nature of the conference, its conclusions and recommendations.

A. Sample Design Specifics

This sampling design is concerned with a 1.4 million acre area
of BLM-administered lands, included in the Twentynine Palms, Johnson/
Morongo, Stoddard, Kramer and Calico planning units, California
Desert (see Figure 1-1). The relevant sampling universe includes
all five planning units, less all parcels not under BLM or State of
California jurisdiction. Because of the comparatively extensive
development within specific areas, especially lands in and near the
Mojave River, Victorville, Barstow, Lucerne Valley, Mojave Valley
and Twentynine Palms, large parcels were entirely excluded from
sampling consideration.

A 0.6% stratified random sample (partially-clustered) of the
above sampling universe was inventoried. This sample consists of
106 sampling units: each unit being one mile long, 1/8 mile wide
and oriented in relation to the existing cadastral system. Each
sampling unit is coterminous with one of sixteen possible zones
(eight running north-south and eight east-west) which cross-partition the idealized one-square mile section. In general, the decision
to orient a given sample unit north-south or east-west was based on
existing contours of elevation; the specific orientation chosen was
that which best followed these contours.

Initially, cadastral sections were evaluated and classified
with respect to two stratifying variables: landform and water
resources. Within each of these, four categories were distinguished:

1. Landform
    a. San Bernardino Mountains
    b. Other Mountains
    c. Valley
    d. Pediment

2. Water Resources
    a. Mojave River
    b. Springs

c. Playa

d. Other Water Resources

These two variables and their respective categories were defined operationally using data available on U.S. Geological Survey topographic maps. These data, together with the existing cadastral system, were used to cross-partition the sampling universe, using the section as the basic unit for partition. Each section was evaluated with respect to each of the stratifying variables; that is, each section was placed in two categories, one for each variable. Thus, for example, a given section might be classified as "valley/playa" or "mountain/spring". To implement the above classification schema, the following set of operational definitions were used.

1. Landform

   a. San Bernardino Mountains - This category included all sections along the southwestern rim of the survey area having a mean elevation of 3500 feet or more. This range is distinguished from other mountain areas because it is marginal to the Mojave Desert and environmentally distinct, and may be archaeologically distinct as well.

   b. Other Mountains - All sections not included in category a. which have an average slope greater than 100 meters/kilometer (10%) were included in this category.

   c. Valley - This category included all sections having an average slope of less than 100 meters/kilometer (10%).

   d. Pediment - Sections lying along the interface between valley and mountain (as defined above) were distinguished as "pediment", but were classified as either valley or mountain based upon the predominant landform within the section.

2. Water Resources

   a. Mojave River - This category included all sections lying within a three-mile zone surrounding the Mojave River.

   b. Springs - Sections were placed in the "spring" category if they contained a recorded spring.

   c. Playa - All sections containing lands identified as "playa" or "dry lake" were placed in this category.

   d. Other Water Resources - This category includes all sections that did not fall in one of the above three categories.

From these two key variables, landform and water resources, five mutually-exclusive sampling domains were identified for study. These were as follows:

1. Mojave River Valley - This domain included all sections class-
    ified in category 2a above, regardless of landform. Mountain
    as well as valley sections were eventually sampled as part of
    this domain.

2. Playa Valleys - This domain included all sections classified
    in category 1c above, which surround playa shorelines (as
    defined in 2c, above) up to a maximum distance of six miles.
    This domain contained no sections classified as "mountain",
    regardless of their proximity to a playa.

3. Spring Areas - All sections classified in category 2b above
    were included in this domain, regardless of landform.

4. Other Valleys - This domain consists of all sections in cate-
    gory 1c above which were not assigned to any of the previous
    domains.

5. Mountains - All sections classified in category 1a above were
    included in this domain.

On the basis of total area representation and estimated relative
archaeological potential, it was decided that three of the five domains
would receive major emphasis in the overall distribution of sampling
units: the Mojave River Valley, Playa Valleys, and Other Valleys.
The Spring and Mountain domains combined were allocated slightly
more than ten percent (thirteen) of the total number of sample units:
seven units were placed within the Spring domain, six in the Mountain
domain. The Mojave River Valley domain was assigned a total of 27
transects (roughly 30% of the grand total), and the Playa Valley
and Other Valley domains combine to make up approximately 60% of
the total (32 and 34 units, respectively).

Somewhat different strategies were used for selecting specific
sample unit locations within the various domains. These strategies
were as follows:

1. Mojave River Valley - Sampling areas within this domain were
    selected on the basis of availability. This resulted from the
    extensive pattern of private land ownership along the river.
    A total of nine areas were eventually located in which three
    consecutive sections, running outward from the river, could
    be sampled. Each of these sets of three sections were included
    in the sample. One unit per section was selected, using the
    same randomly-selected zone number to determine sample unit
    location within each section in the set.

2. Playa Valleys - Within this domain, sampling was conducted by
    the individual playa valley. All available playa valleys were
    included in the sample. A minimum of two and a maximum of
    three units per playa valley were selected. Initially, a
    "chain" of sections, running from the playa shoreline to the
    upper pediment was constructed, as follows:

a. One of the sections along the playa shoreline would be randomly selected.

b. This first section in the chain "touches" eight adjacent sections. From this set of eight, three were identified which lie furthest from the playa, and one of these three was randomly-selected and became the next component of the chain (see Figure 4-1).

c. This selection process continued until the chain of sections reached the foot of a mountain or the arbitrary six mile "Playa Valley" boundary, discussed above was achieved.

Once this chain had been established, the following sampling procedures ensued:

d. One sample unit would be placed in the section at each end of the chain.

e. If there were more than two sections in the chain, one of the remaining sections would be randomly selected to contain a third sample unit.

f. As with the Mojave River Valley sample units, a single random number per valley would be obtained to determine the zone location (within sections) of all sample units, thus creating a series of small systematic cluster samples within the Playa Valley domain.

3. Spring Locations - An initial total of 35 sections containing recorded springs were identified for sampling. From these, seven were randomly selected. Within each section, that zone which included the spring itself became the chosen sampling unit.

4. Other Valleys - Initially, this domain was divided into a series of 17 valleys, based upon topographic features. From this series, 11 were randomly selected for sampling. Sampling within the boundaries of specific valley systems was identical to that for Playa Valleys, except that the section containing the lowest point (in terms of elevation) within the valley became the initial section in the sampling chain.

5. Mountains - Six sample units were selected randomly from the Mountain domain, as described above.

Figures 4-2 through 4-6 provide a general graphic depiction of the locations of the 106 units eventually selected for inclusion in the sample. Appendix IV (unpublished) contains more specific locational information, including place names, map coordinates, and so on.

FIGURE 4-1

Sampling Procedures for Playa Valley Blocks

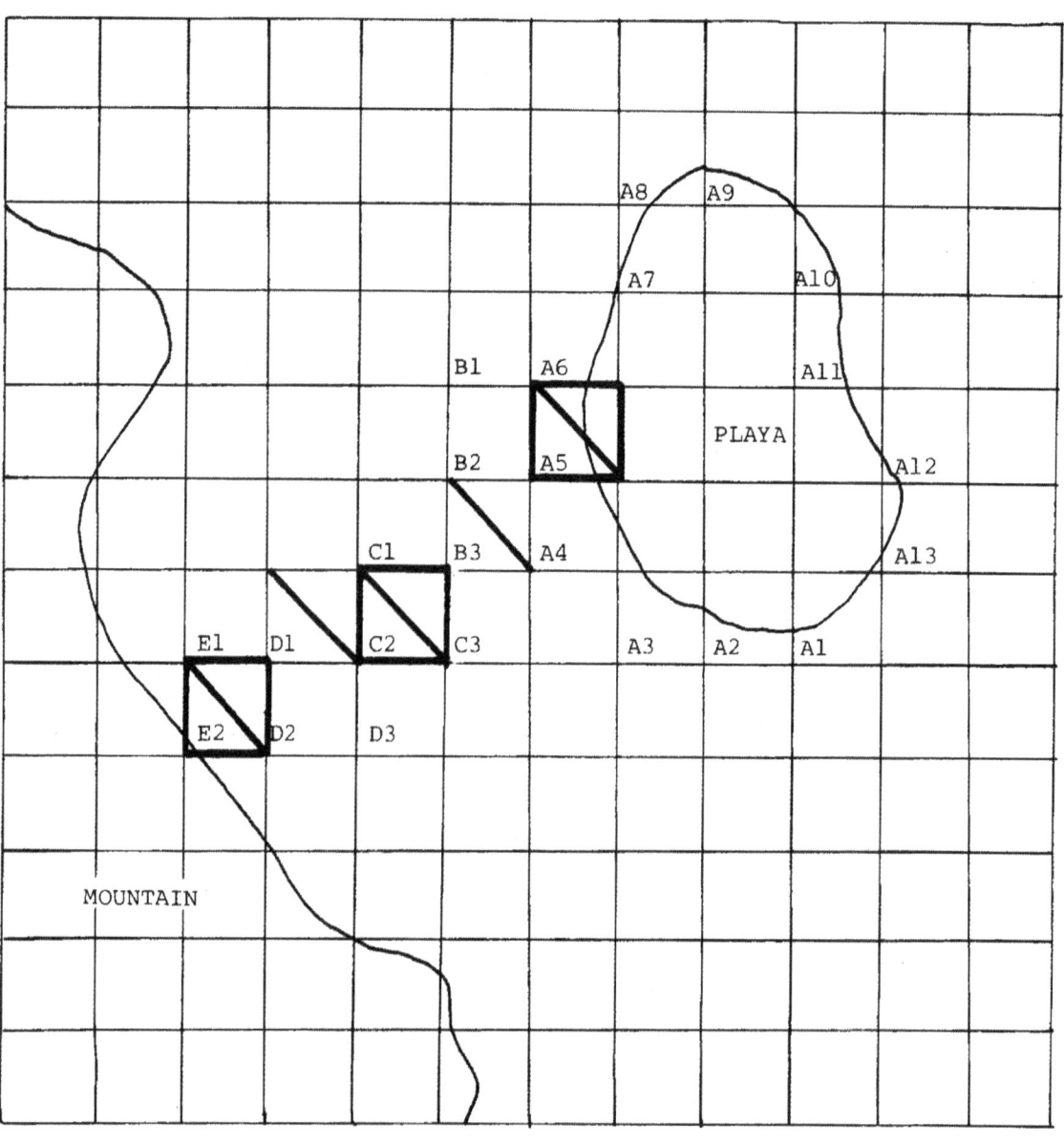

COMMENTARY FOR FIGURE 4-1

Hypothetical Selection Process for "Playa Valley" Transects

Step A. A1-A13 are identified as Playa shoreline; A5 is randomly
         selected from among these to begin the chain.

Step B. B1-B3 are identified as the three sections adjacent to
         A5 lying farthest from the Playa; B3 is randomly selected
         from these and becomes the next section in the chain.

Step C. C1-3 are identified ... (same as above); C2 is selected.
         D1-3 are identified ... (same as above); D1 is selected.
         E1-3 are identified ... (same as above); E2 is selected.

Step D. The chain thus consists of sections A5, B3, C2, D1, and
         E2. A5 and E2 are sampled because they are at the ends
         of the chain.

Step E. One of the remaining sections (B3, C2, D1) is randomly
         selected for sampling. This proves to be C2.

Step F. A single random number is chosen to determine the zone
         location of each sample unit within these three sections.
         A different number is chosen for each individual playa
         valley.

FIGURE 4-2

Calico Planning Unit

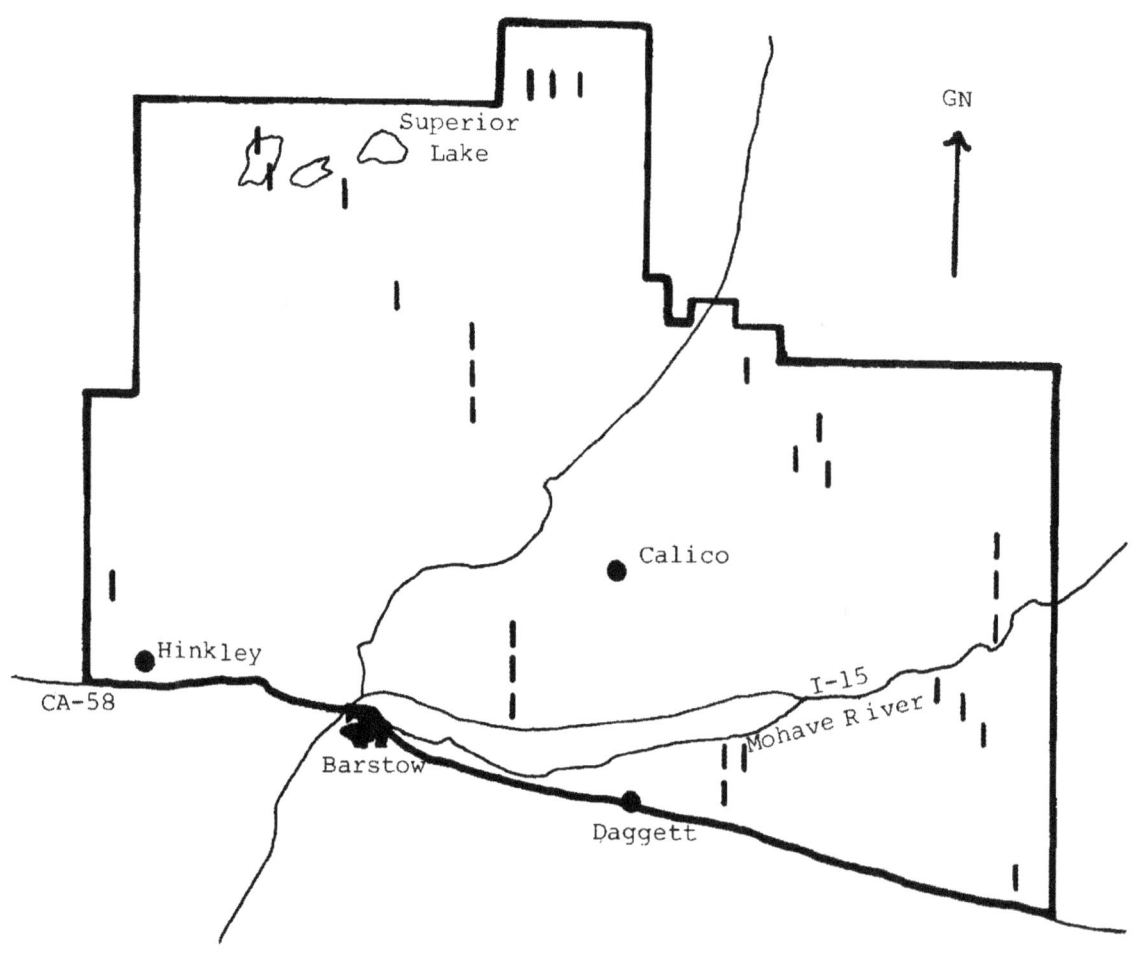

Scale = 1:500,000

FIGURE 4-3

Kramer Planning Unit

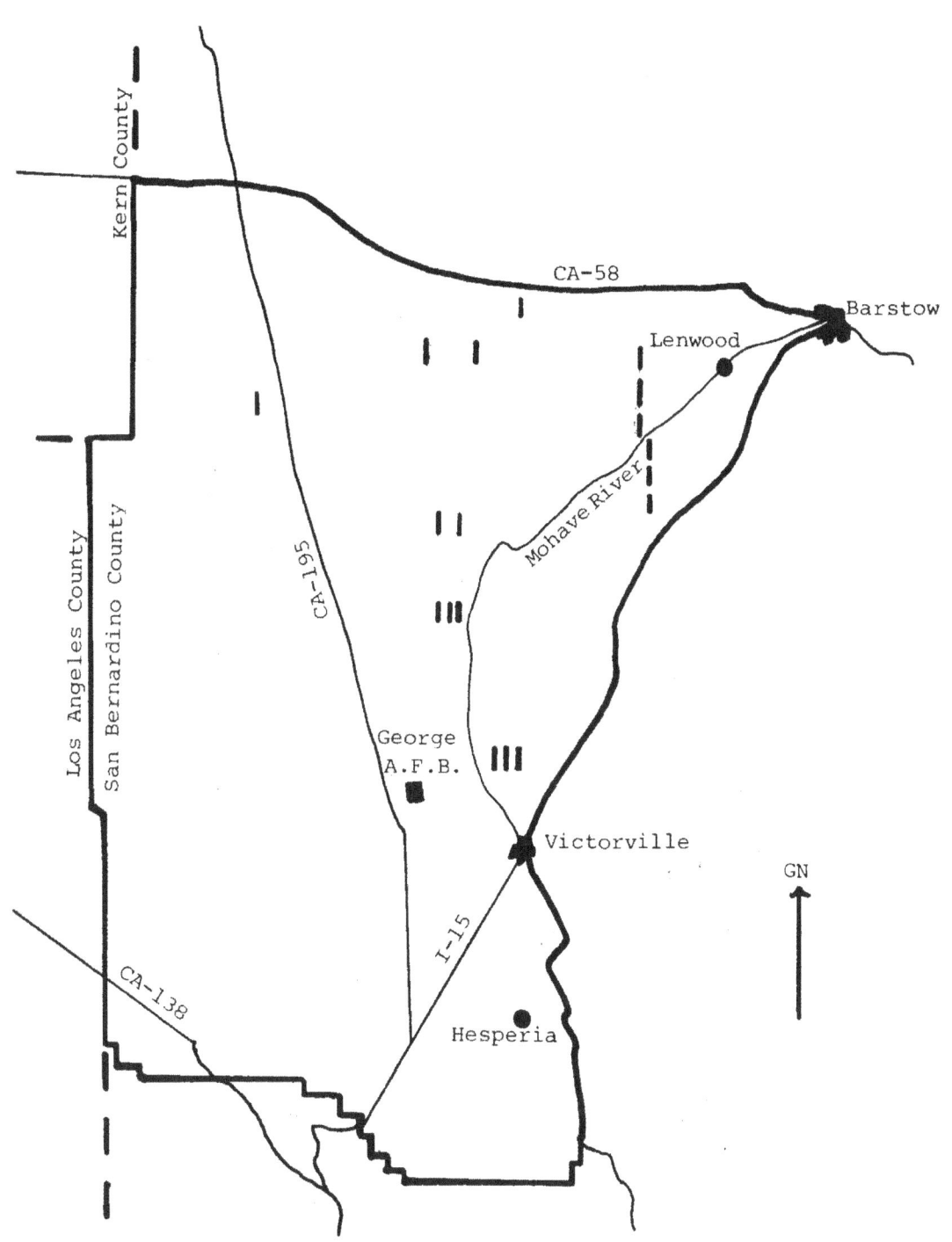

Scale = 1:500,000

FIGURE 4-4

Stoddard Planning Unit

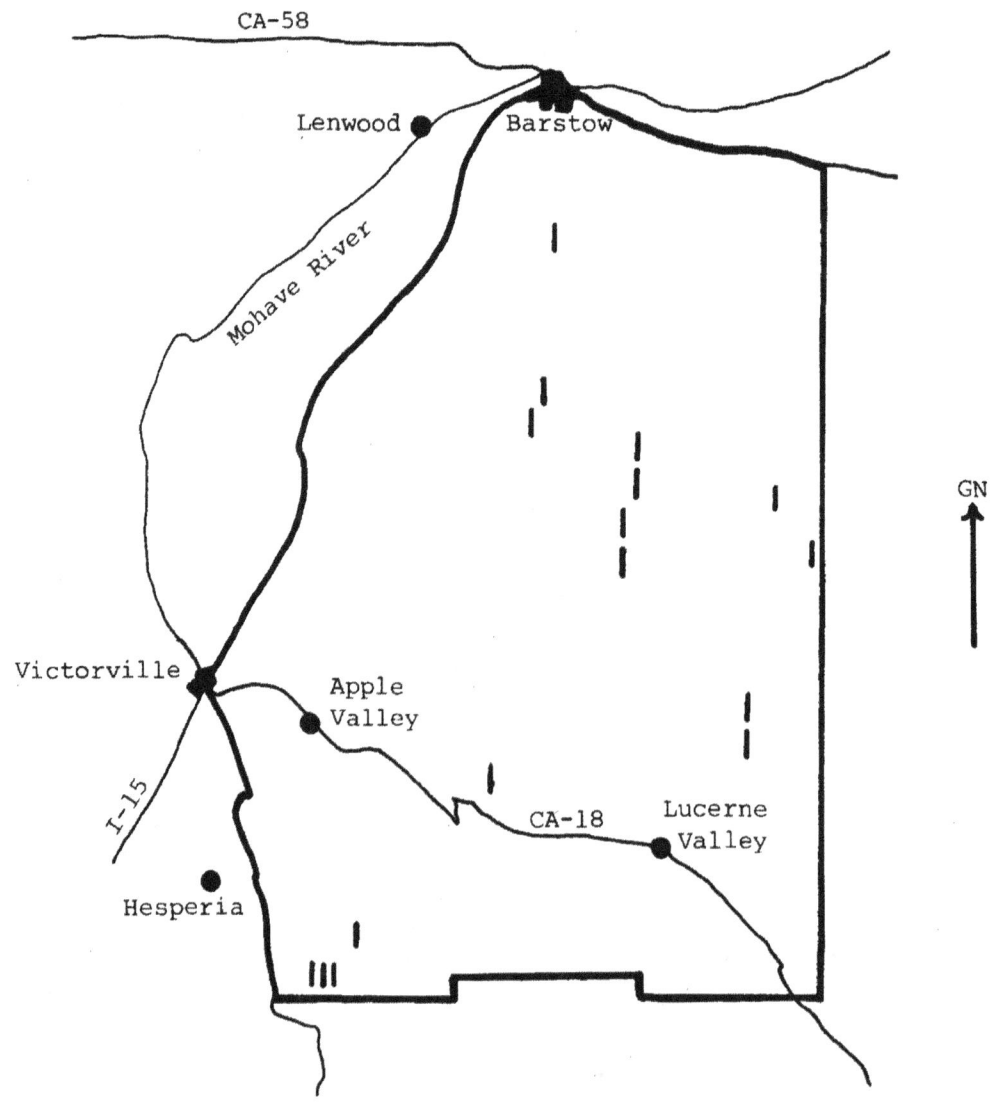

Scale = 1:500,000

FIGURE 4-5

Johnson-Morongo Planning Unit

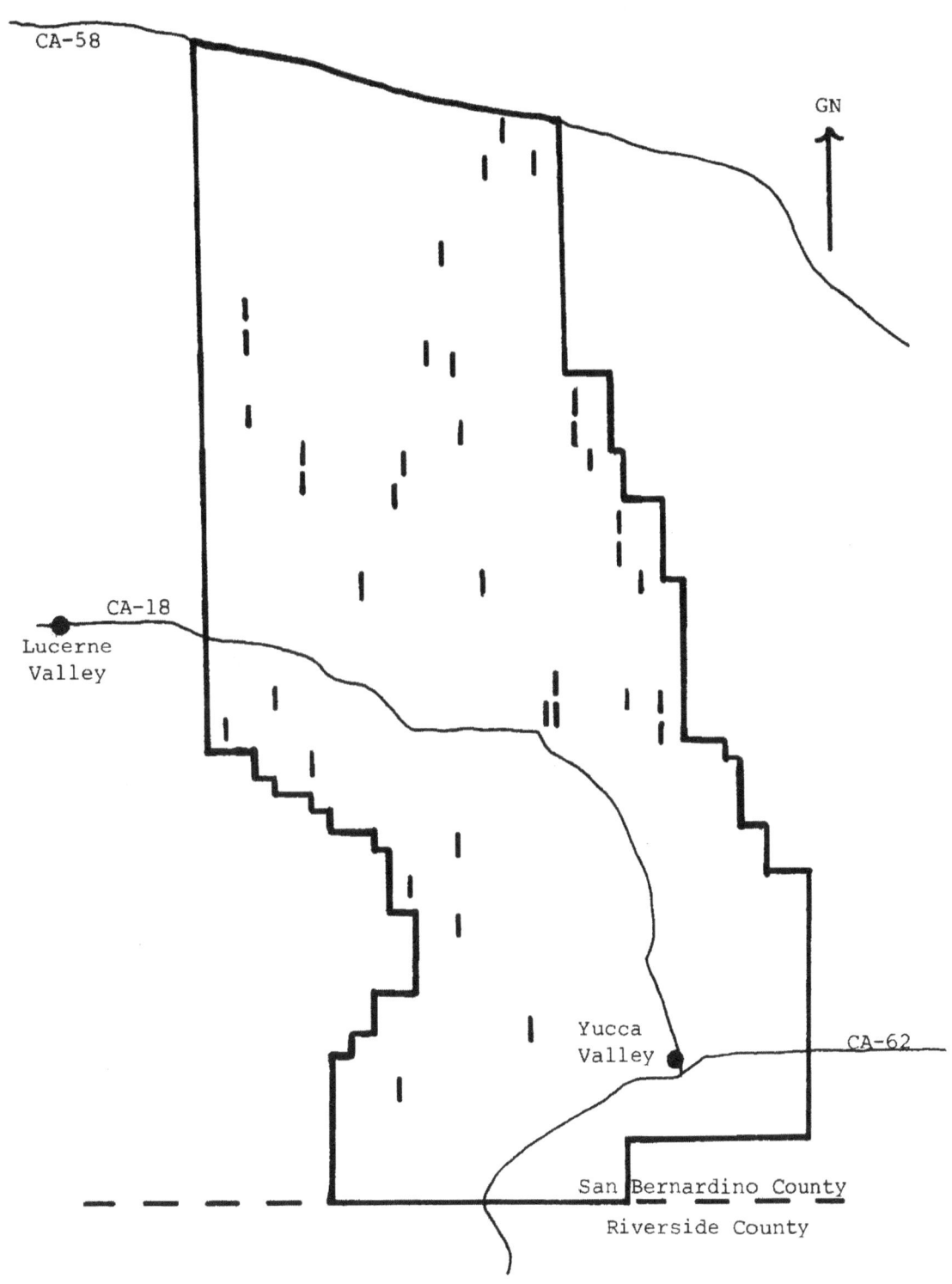

Scale = 1:500,000

FIGURE 4-6

Twentynine Palms Planning Unit

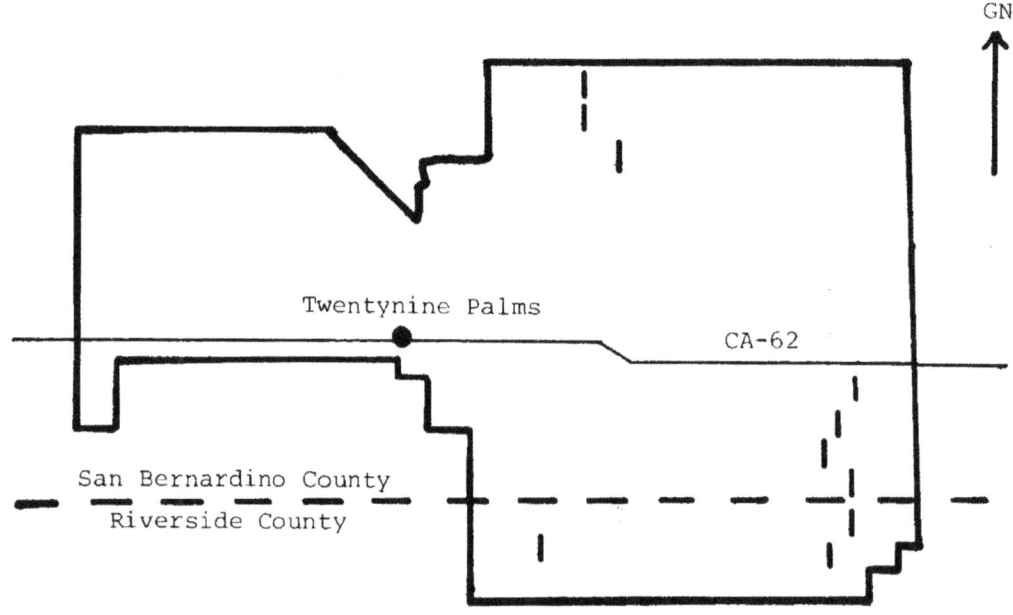

B. Research Design Conference/Rationale

The sampling design outlined above can best be understood in terms of the orientation, conclusions, and recommendations of the July 1-2 Conference. This conference was conducted as an open discussion, with contributions from all present. The resulting decisions were arrived at through formal and informal presentations, discussion, argument (often quite heated), compromise and, finally, general consensus.

Participants in the conference included: Dr. Gary Coombs, project coordinator and Executive Director of ARI; Professors Margaret Lyneis (UNLV), Dwight Read (UCLA), and Claude Warren (UNLV, also President of ARI), and; Elizabeth Warren and Dorothy Ritenour, historical consultants. Also present were six of the eight crew members from the project: Richard McCarty, Field Supervisor; Tara Shepperson and Evan Acker, Crew Chiefs; Cynthia Howell and Kim Geary, Crew Assistants.

The conference began with Dr. Coombs outlining the basic requirements of the contract. He indicated that the BLM was definitely interested in theoretical objectives, in addition to the more basic objectives of identifying site locations and estimating site densities, and suggested that the participants might consider the possibility of focusing on a specific research problem. The group agreed that such a problem focus could probably be selected that would not detract from the other contract requirements.

A variety of possible problem foci were discussed. Dr. Lyneis suggested that it might be very useful to compare valleys with lacustrine systems from other types. The group concluded that this was a workable problem, that it would not adversely affect other project objectives, and that it could lead to significant conclusions that might be applicable to other areas within the California Desert as well. After some discussion, it was decided that the Mojave River Valley should be included as a third valley type, and that spring locations also should be distinguished for examination. The group agreed that it would not be practical to formulate specific hypotheses concerning past human activity in these different environments, but that obviously a variety of such hypotheses could be generated and tested with the resulting data.

In many instances, ARI's research experience in the Northeast Mojave (ARID-I), was used as a comparative backdrop against which to make a variety of decisions. One such decision involved the overall distribution of sample units. Dr. Coombs pointed out that the small size of the Northeast Mojave sample was producing a series of problems in data analysis. Dr. Read reminded the group that a stratified sample should normally emphasize strata in which higher site frequencies are expected, and asked whether any assumptions could be made, prior to the inventory, concerning where sites tended to be located. It was agreed that most desert work, including ARI's

Northeast Mojave project, indicated that site densities tended to be particularly low in steep-gradient areas, and the suggestion was made that such areas be excluded from sampling consideration. Richard McCarty questioned the advisability of making this low-density assumption for mountainous areas, particularly in light of the exploratory nature of the present work. Eventually, after much heated discussion, it was agreed that while it may not be reasonable to assume that past human activity in the Western Mojave mountains was not unlike that in other California Desert regions, it was quite reasonable to conclude that a sufficiently large sample was unavailable for even testing this assumption. On this basis, it was decided that all mountain sample units should be concentrated in the flanks of the San Bernardino Mountains, lying along the southwestern border of the project area, since these stand out as differing in a variety of ways from other desert ranges.

The issue of dispersed versus clustered sampling was also discussed. The principal argument against clustering emphasized its relatively high cost (in terms of the allocation of sample units) and the resultant loss in broad coverage. Conversely, it was pointed out that dispersed samples provided little information concerning the patterning of sites and could create analytical problems in efforts to identify meaningful relationships between site locations and environmental variables (this too was exemplified by the Northeast Mojave project). Finally, a compromise was reached when it was agreed to limit clustering to a portion of the total sample (i.e. spring and mountain units would not be clustered) and to a maximum of three sample units per cluster.

A final issue involved the possible structuring of sample units within clusters. Dr. Coombs reported that the Block Sampling technique used in the ARID-I project, which used structured clusters to examine site patterning across valleys, was providing valuable information that may have broad applications throughout the California Desert (see Coombs 1978). The group decided that this type of structuring would not adversely effect the other positive aspects of the clustering approach, and it was agreed to incorporate it into the sampling design.

CHAPTER 5. FIELD IMPLEMENTATION

Sharon Dean and Gary Coombs

A. The Field Experience

Since the field portion of ARID-II was performed during the
extreme heat of summer, the work was conducted from a series of
towns where motel accommodations could be found. The length of
stay in any given location ranged from two to eleven days, depending upon the number of sample units within reasonable access of
the base location. Bases were chosen so as to minimize distances
to a maximum number of sample units. Generally speaking, there
was little time for "settling in" so living was out of boxes and
baggage. The number of people per motel room ranged from two to
four, but with adjoining rooms in several places there was a considerable amount of social exchange between crew members.

Meals were generally eaten out since cooking facilities were
seldom available. Crew members usually took one common meal per
day in a local restaurant; "junk" food, fruits, salads, cheese and
various other cold foods made up the balance of the diet. The
cold drink consumption was of phenomenal proportion.

The work day began early in order to avoid the midday heat.
The time of departure each morning was determined relative to the
distance to that day's sample units, as well as road conditions
and estimated "walk-in" time. On most days, the goal of leaving
the field before noon meant being on the road by 4:00 AM. After-
noon and evening hours were spent completing forms and preparing
equipment, material, and crews for the following day's work.

Heat-induced lethargy and boredom were constant problems.
Consequently, most of the crew members slept a good deal during the
hot afternoons and picked up work again in the latter part of the
day. Recreation consisted of swimming (whenever we had access to
a pool), an occasional movie ("Star Wars" played everywhere), and
a few trips to local museums. Much leisure time was spent reading.

Work was carried out in ten day periods with four day breaks.
This schedule permitted crew members the time for long drives home
on weekends; Las Vegas residents to pools and air-conditioning
and Santa Barbarans to the beach.

Transportation to and from the field each day was by private
vehicle as well as ARI's new yellow "Brat" which was broken-in on
this project. Mechanical problems were non-existent, and the Brat
performed so well that we probably should have been filmed for an
auto industry commercial.

Despite the intense heat, the climate was, for the most part, quite favorable. There were only one or two days when winds were uncomfortably strong and, though a rainstorm threatened, the only actual rain occurred on one of our four-day breaks.

B. Personnel

For the entire span of fieldwork four 2-member crews were utilized. The individuals participating in the fieldwork were: R. McCarty (Field Supervisor); T. Shepperson, E. Acker and U. Klymyshyn (Crew Chiefs); and S. Dean, C. Howell, P. Rocchio, and K. Geary (Crew Members). Eric Ritter of the BLM Desert Planning Staff joined the crew for a brief period, providing valuable input to the field effort. Eric also provided a welcome diversion from routine by taking the crew to visit some petroglyph sites near Black Mountain one evening.

C. Standard Inventory Procedures

As described in Chapter 4, sample units were one mile long, 1/8 mile wide and oriented either north-south or east-west. In general, the following methods were employed to inventory each sample unit:

1. The sample unit would be traversed lengthwise, on foot, by a two person crew. The crew would include the crew chief and his/her assistant. The crew chief would carry a map and compass and would be responsible for the overall orientation of the crew in relation to the sample unit.

2. The crews would also carry a 35mm camera, loaded with color slide film, at least one canteen of water, rations (generally cheese, fruits, or "trail mix"), a clipboard and full set of inventory forms, and writing and plotting instruments.

3. Crew members would be spaced approximately fifty meters apart, with pacing used to determine the initial fify meter separation. The crew chief's assistant would be responsible for maintaining this interval during the course of the survey; this would normally be accomplished by visual inspection or, when necessary, by re-pacing.

4. Two generally-parallel sweeps were necessary for one crew to cover one sample unit. Normally, these sweeps would move in opposite directions to one another (see Figure 1-2, which describes the idealized survey path).

5. Initial access to the unit was usually obtained by a combination of vehicular travel followed by travel on foot up to a distance of several miles. In a number of instances, the sample unit was more or less directly accessible by vehicle.

6. Since the sample units were initially defined in terms of map coordinates, it was necessary for the crews to a) locate the

corresponding position on the ground and b) successfully navigate the sample unit as it had been defined. A combination of several basic techniques were generally employed to accomplish these tasks. The techniques involved included the use of:

a. Map reference points, such as section markers, mountain peaks, buildings and roads;

b. Vehicle odometer readings coupled with map distances;

c. Map resection, a survey technique in which compass azimuths (i.e. directions) to three or more visible, known landmarks are used to determine the (map) position of the observer;

d. Back-sighting, a simplified form of resection in which the back (compass) azimuth to one visible landmark is used to determine the distance traversed along an assumed course of fixed azimuth.

7. At least one color slide would be taken of the sample unit. Normally this would be done at or near that end of the unit which afforded the best lighting and topographic conditions to yield a representative view of as much as possible of the sample unit. All photographs were recorded on a BLM Photographic Record Form (see Appendix II).

8. The ARID-II project area is characterized by a variety of site types, and it is apparent that each type can best be seen using a particular kind of observational technique (For example, isolated chipped stone artifacts are comparatively small and difficult to see; thus they are most readily observed with one's vision fixed at a relatively short distance. In contrast, large features such as cairns or hearths could be found in greater frequency by employing a somewhat broader scanning technique). Accordingly, crew members were instructed to vary their scanning methods as a means of avoiding grossly disproportionate observations of different site types.

9. Minimum site criteria were as follows: one artifact, cultural feature, or waste flake was considered to be a site; only materials considered to be post-World War II were excluded from site recording. Upon locating a site, the survey sweep would be halted and both members of the crew would participate in site recording. This would include the taking of photographs (particularly if the site were unusual in relation to previously recorded sites), plotting of the site on a U.S. Geological Survey map (this generally required the same techniques as described in 6. above for sample unit location and navigation), and the preparation of the appropriate BLM Site Survey forms (this involved recording information concerning biogeographical and other aspects of the natural environment, as well as information relating to the extant cultural remains and locational data (see Appendix II). Where appropriate, sites were mapped and artifact

-43-

drawings were made. Upon the completion of site recording the survey sweep would resume as before. No collecting was undertaken.

10. Sites were recorded whether they fell within the limits of a sample unit or not. In particular, a number of sites were observed and recorded in the process of accessing the sample units themselves. Since there was no way to maintain a systematic control over the amount of area covered off sample units, special care was taken to differentiate sites recorded on versus those recorded off the sample units.

11. Upon completion of each sample unit, a BLM Sample Unit Record would be prepared by the crew. Like the Site Survey Records, the Sample Unit Record contains information concerning both the natural and cultural characteristics of the sample unit (see Appendix II).

12. Crews would collect field specimens of lithic materials (unmodified) or plant species which they could not fully identify. These would be classified upon returning to base camp, either by members of other crews or with the aid of a variety of field manuals.

D. Deviations from Typical Inventory Methods

Occasionally it was found necessary to deviate from the above-outlined procedures. The following represent some of the most common types of variant procedures.

1. Frequently, portions of the site and sample unit record forms would not be completed until the crew had returned from the field. This was particularly likely when time, heat, or other constraints limited the period the crew could remain in the field, or when classification of cultural or natural items required consultation with other crew members or reference materials.

2. Occasionally, when proximity of sample units permitted, two crews would combine and initiate a 4-person sweep pattern. This pattern was begun at the center of the sample unit with two 2-person crews walking in opposite directions to the ends of the unit. This pattern proved to be most effective in areas where the "Brat" could be driven to the center of the sample unit, and was employed when extremely high temperatures or the late hour made a shortened exposure time desirable.

3. In a few instances it proved impossible to inventory all of the surface area of a particular sample unit. Steep terrain and the presence of water or other physical obstacles were generally the determining factors involved. In these cases, territory adjoining the original sample unit was substituted and surveyed as if it were the sample unit.

CHAPTER 6. VALIDITY AND RELIABILITY

This chapter is concerned with the validity and reliability of the research procedures developed and utilized in ARID-II. In the report on the Northeast Mojave (Coombs 1978), these concepts were defined and discussed at great length. Rather than reiterate that discussion here, I will briefly review its main points and the reader may refer to the earlier report if more detailed explanations are desired.

The concept of validity deals with what a particular research tool accomplishes. We may question the validity of practically any instrument; be it an operational definition, a measurement device, formal logic, or an entire research design. "In each case, validity refers to the degree to which the tool under examination does what we want it to" (Coombs 1978: 58). An instrument is invalid when it does not accomplish these desired goals.

Reliability is generally concerned with the variability produced in the process of replicating a particular measurement. Two basic types of reliability can be distinguished: observational reliability and sampling reliability. Observational reliability involves efforts to re-perform one or more observations. Suppose, for example, that we attempted to re-survey a given ARID-II sample unit. What factors might lead to different results being recorded? Since our navigational techniques are imprecise, for example, we might end up covering a slightly different piece of territory. If a different crew were employed, their greater or lesser expertise in locating sites might also make a difference. Differences in weather conditions or time of day might facilitate or hinder our efforts in relation to our first attempt. Any factor which produces variability in observational results reflects adversely upon the reliability of our observational techniques.

In the case of sampling reliability, the following question is posed: If a new set of sample units were selected, using the same sampling design, would we still reach the same analytical conclusions concerning the sampling universe? Problems of sampling reliability are generally handled through statistical testing; the confidence level associated with most statistical results should tell us the probability that those results are a by-product of sampling error. Each form of reliability is thus closely tied to the concept of "measurement error" and to the elimination or control of irrelevant, exogenous or chance influences which produce undesirable fluctuations in measurement results.

In summary, validity is concerned with what a given research tool accomplishes, while reliability deals with the consistency with which the tool performs its task. It is crucial to understand that these functions are closely interdependent in the sense that one is practically worthless without the other; a tool cannot be valid if it is unreliable and reliability is worthless if the tool does not accomplish its stated purpose. The remainder of this chapter will discuss how these two concepts relate to the ARID-II research.

A. Validity

I would like to address my discussion of the validity of the ARID-II research to two main topics: measurement systems and analytical procedures.

1. Measurement Validity

In an analogous chapter in the ARID-I report (Coombs 1978), I identified a number of potential or real problems associated with the measurement of environmental and cultural resource variables. With regard to the former, I pointed out that the analysis dealt exclusively with contemporary measurements of environmental variables and that many of these were made over a single desert season. The same is true for the ARID-II environmental measures. The validity problem rests in the assumption that these measures may be applied to past environments in a static fashion. Obviously, the problem is most severe in the case of the more transient elements of the present environment (e.g. vegetation and water resources) and far less so for the more stable elements (e.g. general landform). This is not an easily corrected problem. Since the ARID-II analysis is based on these contemporary, seasonal measurements, it is important (for the reader as well as the researcher) to remain cognizant of the inherent problems. I will have occasion to refer to this validity question in the following chapter, when I discuss the results of the analysis.

The validity problem involved in measuring cultural resources takes two basic forms. The first type of problem is most directly related to research oriented toward theory-building or culture-historic reconstruction. Quite obviously, if one is interested in the pattern of past human activity and/or the underlying determinants of that pattern, then any factor which acts to obliterate a portion of the record of past activity is undesirable. Among a whole series of problems, such factors will act to disguise meaningful relationships which once existed involving the forms and spatial distributions of behavior.

The second type of problem related to the measurement of cultural resources concerns the management and preservation of those resources and is somewhat more complicated. If one is concerned only with recording the attributes and locations of existing sites, there is little problem here, since the inventory process performs these measurements directly. Such a record is valuable from a management standpoint, of course, since it provides concrete information about a specific set of resources which can then be protected. This, however, is almost necessarily a very small sample of the existing resources (as in ARID-I), and it is thus important to attempt to make area-wide predictions based on this sample. As in the case of research geared toward historical reconstruction or theoretical concerns, this task is generally accomplished by identifying associations, within the sample, between cultural resources on the one hand and environmental or other independent variables on the other. Unless the investigation is very successful in controlling for the types of measurement biases outlined above, many associations will be missed in the analysis (and perhaps artificial ones will be created) and predictive accuracy will be lost. In my discussion of the patterning of sites in the Mojave River Valley, I will briefly allude to a possible example of this problem. In short, regardless of the orientation of the research, the differential preservation of cultural resources will have an important adverse effect on the validity of the conclusions that are ultimately reached.

A much more concrete problem associated with site measurement involves crew spacing. In the ARID-I report, I pointed out that the 50-meter spacing used between crew members led inevitably to the under-recording of sites within sample units. I indicated that this would be biased especially against small sites and those which do not extend significantly above the ground surface. The effects of terrain and vegetation cover were also discussed, together with possible remedies. These same problems apply to the ARID-II fieldwork. Partially because of this set of problems, I have elected not to include quantitative (i.e. absolute) estimates of site frequencies in this report (see Chapter 7).

2. Analytical Validity

In some ways, the ARID-II data set proves to be an analytical nightmare. Since it includes structured-clusters (i.e. "blocks") of sample units, it is neither a pure random sample nor even a simple stratified sample. Accordingly, in many cases, a simple comparison of transects cannot be used to reach statistically valid conclusions.

I have dealt with this and related problems in a variety of different analytical ways. Rather than detail these here, I will defer discussion until I discuss the analysis itself. I wanted to discuss this point here, however, because it is very easy to use statistical methods which are grossly invalid given the idiosyncrasies of the ARID-II sample. In particular, it is essential to avoid treating transects within blocks as independent and equivalent observations. Hopefully, this will serve as an adequate caution to future researchers who would like to work with these data.

B. Reliability

At the beginning of this chapter, I described two types of reliability - sampling reliability and observational reliability. I indicated that sampling reliability is controlled for through the analytical techniques that a researcher employs and the measures of statistical probability that are associated with these techniques. Thus, sampling reliability becomes a problem only when invalid analytical methods are applied.

Earlier in this chapter, I listed a series of factors which I felt could conceivably affect observational reliability. This list included: weather conditions, time of day, navigational problems and crew composition. Most of these were discussed and evaluated in detail in the ARID-I report (Coombs 1978); the reader should refer to this earlier report for more information. Here, I would like to concentrate on crew composition and its possible impact on the ARID-II survey results.

Individuals obviously differ in terms of their abilities to observe and record archaeological sites. Moreover, this variability undoubtedly increases if one differentiates between site types. If it can be shown that there exists a significant amount of variability in observational skills within the membership of a particular field crew, then it becomes important to control for this undesirable influence on the survey data. Accordingly, I tested to determine if this variation existed within the ARID-II fieldwork.

Each sample unit was categorized by 1) the crew chief involved and 2) whether or not any sites were recorded. Various comparisons were made involving control for stratification category, block, and so on. None of the tests revealed statistically significant differences between crews. However, the results repeatedly pointed toward a single ordering of crews in terms of their relative success in finding sites, and this ordering agreed perfectly with my subjective impressions of the relative abilities of each crew chief as a survey archaeologist. This finding has convinced me that real differences exist between these individuals/crews in terms of their observational skills. Nevertheless, the empirical differences were so small that I felt there was no need to control for crew composition through the remainder of the analysis.

C. Summary and Conclusions

In this chapter, I have identified what I feel are the more critical validity and reliability problems confronting the ARID-II research. This has been a comparatively brief review, because most of the topics touched upon here have been dealt with extensively in the ARID-I report (Coombs 1978).

Some of the problems outlined above have been described but not controlled for in the analysis. In large part, this deficiency

stems from the limited resources available to this research, and
the sometimes detailed analytical measures that are required to
implement such controls. I think it is important to mention these
problems, however, even if nothing further is done about them,
for two basic reasons. First, it gives the reader a somewhat
better vantage point from which to interpret the analytical results
and other conclusions which I will present. The reader should now
have a clearer understanding of the assumptions underlying the
analysis and potential problems with those assumptions. The reader
now knows what has "bothered" me about the ARID-II data and may be
able to more easily identify other factors which should have concerned me. In short, this discussion should provide a means for
developing a more critical (and valid) evaluation of the remainder
of this report. Secondly, this discussion may hopefully give some
archaeologists a few new ideas about how to organize a research
program. The mistakes and successes of ARID-II each has something
to contribute here.

CHAPTER 7. RESULTS

In this chapter, the results of the analytical portion of the ARID-II research will be presented, together with the conclusions resulting from this analysis. Since this is a relatively lengthy chapter, I will begin by outlining the various chapter topics.

First, the primary objectives of the analysis will be discussed. Secondly, I will describe the basic strategy that was used to meet these objectives. Thirdly, the more crucial features of the raw data collected during the research will be described. Fourthly, the analytical results themselves will be detailed, including any theoretical conclusions that may be derived from them. Finally, I will review these results, identifying questions that remain unanswered and suggesting possible avenues for further research in the California Desert in general and the Western Mojave in particular.

A. Objectives

The basic objectives of the analysis phase of ARID-II perhaps can be summed up best in the form of two simply-stated questions:

1. Where are the cultural resources located within the study area?

2. Why are they located where they are?

The first question is by far the more fundamental of the two. Basically, it involves the correct identification of associations or relationships between site data on the one hand and environmental and locational data on the other, and the use of these observed associations in the prediction of overall cultural resource numbers and distributions patterns, in either relative or absolute form. Answering this question serves the management goal of the research most directly since it may be used to make decisions concerning the relative sensitivity, and archaeological and historical potential of different sub-regions and so on.

While the second question above is directly dependent upon the first, it goes much further in the sense that it requires that the relationships between site and environmental patterns be tied to more-or-less explicit theoretical arguments. Unlike the first question, it should lead to insights which reflect the theoretical dimension of the research. This latter objective, however, serves the management goal as well. As pointed out in the ARID-I research report (Coombs 1978), when site predictions are based simply on numerical or other "correlations", when they are not developed with a sensitivity toward theoretical concerns, it is very easy to confuse spurious relationships (e.g. patterns created by sampling error) with real ones. This discrimination is critical, from the management standpoint, if only because the latter type of relationship alone will lead to accurate predictions and extrapolations. Efforts toward linking observed relationships with theoretical arguments cannot guarantee, of course, a perfect differentiation between the real and the spurious; but any progress in this direction is generally a valuable contribution. In this sense, even research projects which are addressed only to the prediction of site locations and patterns should include a theoretical component.

Many archaeologists feel that contract research does not permit the degree of attention to theory that most of us would like to see. Hopefully, these arguments may aid in some small way toward making theoretical concerns an integral part of management-oriented archaeology. Hopefully, too, this report will reflect the value of such an approach.

B. Approach

The analytical approach used in ARID-II has been based on a number of decisions concerning how to best meet the stated objectives:

1. As in ARID-I, the analysis of the Western Mojave data predominantly involved a comparison of sample units rather than of sites. While analysis by the site can potentially identify differences in the distribution of different site types, it was concluded that there were two few sites of distinct types and too little time available to make such an approach significantly valuable. Additionally, analysis by the site cannot lead directly to accurate density and distributional estimates, since there is no way to determine where sites are absent. Analysis by the sample unit permits such controls since a portion of the units contain no sites.

2. The analysis deals only with sites recorded within sample unit boundaries; sites recorded outside of the transects can contribute relatively little to the analysis, since there is no easy means of determining area coverage. Additionally, only a handful of sites (4) were recorded outside of transects in the Western Mojave study area. This differs significantly from the Northeast Mojave (24% of the ARID-I sites were recorded off transects; less than 4% for ARID-II). This may be attributed, perhaps to the comparative abundance of roads in the Western Mojave and the resultant drop in the average walking distance required to reach a sample unit.

3. In the ARID-I analysis, a series of estimates were generated for the overall archaeological potential of the project area as a whole, as well as for various specific environmental zones. These estimates included predictions of actual site frequencies together with projected probabilities of locating sites within a sample unit randomly selected from a given

zone. While these were "best estimates" in a statistical sense they were nevertheless highly speculative. I have come to feel that these estimates actually may be counter-productive to the development of the BLM Desert Plan, in that they seem to say a lot when they actually say relatively little.

In the case of the Western Mojave, for example, this estimation process would lead to the conclusion that there were no historic sites in the "Other Valley" stratum (since 34 sample units failed to reveal any historic sites). Obviously this would be an underestimate, and it would be a most dangerous one. In order to avoid this problem to the maximum extent possible, the ARID-II analysis is geared almost exclusively toward the generation of relative estimates, linking postulated differences in site numbers or densities with environmental or locational differences. This should serve as the best source of information for making relative decisions concerning the futures of different regions within the Western Mojave. Nevertheless, Table 7-1 incorporates density estimates for both prehistoric and historic sites, within each of the sampling strata. The reader should understand that these estimates are quite unreliable, due largely to the small ARID-II sample proportion, and thus should be applied only with considerable caution.

4. Finally, it was concluded that the ARID-II analysis should be relatively simple in design; thus the analysis focuses on a comparatively small number of topic variables. These were selected largely on the basis of the results of the Research Design Conference and the ARID-I research; variables incorporated here included those which proved of significance in the Northeast Mojave as well as those which seemed essential to answering questions posed at the Western Mojave Conference. In this sense, the ARID-II analysis was designed, in part, to answer questions of significance not only to the Western Mojave but to other parts of the California Desert as well.

With the exception of a few t-tests and other simple statistics, the analysis was performed on Archaeological Research's Tandy TRS-80 microcomputer. This system includes a version of the BASIC programming language, over 22,000 bytes of memory available for programs and data, and a mini-disk for storage and retrieval.

The following statistical routines were designed specifically for the ARID-II analysis:

1. Stepwise Regression - handles up to 15 variables, with various options concerning the introduction of independent variables to the regression equation; it will base calculations on all or part of a total data set and generates a variety of supporting statistics

2. Analysis of Covariance - a simple one-way version with diagnostic statistics

TABLE 7-1A

The Distribution of Prehistoric Sites
by Stratification Category

Stratification Category	Number of Sample Units	Total Number of Sites Recorded	Proportion of Sample Units Containing Sites	Sites per Sample Unit	Variance	Est. Number of Sites per Square Mile
PLAYA VALLEYS	32	15				
Zone 1	11	11	0.36	1.0	2.6	8.0
Zone 2	9	0	0	0	0	0
Zone 3	12	4	0.25	0.33	0.4	2.7
MOJAVE RIVER VALLEY	27	50				
Zone 1	9	12	0.78	1.33	1.5	10.7
Zone 2	9	25	0.44	2.78	15.7	22.2
Zone 3	9	13	0.33	1.44	7.0	11.6
OTHER VALLEYS	34	57				
Zone 1	12	4	0.17	0.33	0.08	2.7
Zone 2	11	27	0.27	2.45	17.17	19.6
Zone 3	11	26	0.18	2.36	30.85	18.9
SPRINGS	7	6	0.57	0.86	1.14	6.9
MOUNTAINS	6	2	0.33	0.33	0.27	2.7
ALL STRATA	106	130				

TABLE 7-1B

The Distribution of Historic Sites
by Stratification Category

Stratification Category	Number of Sample Units	Total Number of Sites Recorded	Proportion of Sample Units Containing Sites	Sites per Sample Unit	Variance	Est. Number of Sites per Square Mile
Playa Valleys	32	1	0.07	0.03	0.03	0.25
Mojave River Valley	34	2	0.06	0.06	0.06	0.47
Other Valleys	27	0	0	0	0	0
Springs	7	3	0.29	0.43	0.62	3.4
Mountains	6	1	0.17	0.17	0.17	1.3
All Strata	106	7				

3. Kendall's Tau - computes the rank order correlation

In addition, the following routines, developed for ARID-I, were also used:

1. Crosstabulation - cross tabulates two or three variables. This program was updated to permit the user to control for a fourth variable

2. Regression/Correlation - performs simple (linear) regression, Pearson Correlation, tri-variate regression and partial correlation, bivariate plots and significance measures

3. Spearman's r - computes the rank order correlation

4. Analysis of Variance - one and two-way versions. The latter may be used when cell frequencies are unequal, employing an approximation detailed by Walker and Lev (1953: 381-382).

5. Fisher's Exact Test - computes exact probabilities for 2 x 2 contingency tables

C. The Basic Data

This section briefly describes the principal characteristics of the data collected during the ARID-II fieldwork. Since it is impractical to outline all of the data, or even to present it in a manner suited to most purposes, I have attempted to select and arrange the data in a fashion which seems generally to do the best job of providing a sound, overall view.

The environmental variables used in the analysis included the following:

1. Vegetation

    a. distance to nearest juniper/piñon stand
    b. presence/absence of yucca/joshua in the sample unit
    c. distance to nearest mesquite

2. Water Resources

    a. distance to Mojave River
    b. distance to nearest spring
    c. distance to nearest playa
    d. distance to valley floor

3. Geophysical and Other

    a. stratification category
    b. valley width
    c. valley contour (distance to valley floor divided by valley width and other related composites)

d. block
e. block position
f. elevation

The analysis examined different site types and site components as well as pooled site categories.

Table 7-1 details the distribution of sites by each of the five stratification categories. The table is divided into two parts; Part A deals with prehistoric sites and Part B treats historic sites. A number of diagnostic statistics are incorporated into the Table, including the proportion of sample units which contained sites, mean site frequencies per sample unit, and estimated site densities per square mile (the reader is again cautioned regarding the speculative nature of these latter estimates). Since the three valley strata (i.e. "Playa", "Mojave River", and "Other") contain clustered sub-samples (i.e. blocks), it would be incorrect to simply pool these results together. Instead, within each of the valley strata, sample units have been differentiated by block-location. Specifically, Zone 1 in the table refers to those sample units located nearest the valley floor (within each block) while Zones 2 and 3 refer to those located intermediate and furthest from the valley floor, respectively (this differentiation has been performed only in Part A of Table 7-1, since so few historic sites were recorded during the inventory).

Table 7-2 presents the raw frequencies for the various prehistoric and historic site types found both within and outside of the 106 sample units. Ten different prehistoric site types and 130 prehistoric sites in total were recorded within transects during the ARID-II fieldwork. Additionally, a total of seven historic sites were recorded within transects, for a grand total of 137 recorded sites lying within sample unit boundaries. Only four sites (all prehistoric) were recorded outside of the transects.

Table 7-3 concentrates specifically on the prehistoric sites. The Table describes the numbers of recorded sites which contained each of ten site components. Of course many sites contained several of these components; thus multiple entries are recorded. Once again, sites recorded within transects have been distinguished from those lying outside transect boundaries.

Table 7-4, which is divided into seven parts, illustrates the distribution of sample units by stratification category and by seven key environmental variables. Within each environmental variable, category limits have been set at equal intervals and the number of categories per variable has been selected to provide the most descriptive and efficient range possible.

D. Analytical Findings

Earlier in this chapter, it was indicated that the analysis of the ARID-II data would not be geared toward the generation of _abso-_

TABLE 7-2

Number of Sites by Site Type
Within and Off Sample Units

SITE TYPE:

Prehistoric Site Types	On Sample Units	Off Sample Units
Isolated Find	42	2
Lithic Scatter	60	1
Temporary Camp	14	1
Milling Station	3	0
Shelter-Cave	2	0
Pottery Locus	1	0
Rock Alignment	2	0
Cairn	1	0
Quarry Site	3	1
Other	2	0
Total	130	5
Historic Site Types		
Mine	3	0
Homestead	1	0
Unknown	3	0
Total	7	0
Grand Total	137	5

TABLE 7-3

Numbers of Sites Containing Each of 10 Prehistoric Site
Components Within and Off Sample Units

Prehistoric Sites Containing:	NUMBER OF SITES	
	On Sample Units	Off Sample Units
Flake Scatters	94	4
Points	4	0
Other Chipped Stone	63	1
Ground Stone	5	0
Pottery	2	0
Shelter-Cave	2	0
Rock Circles, Alignments, Clearings	4	0
Hearths, Fire-cracked Rock	11	0
Cairns	2	0

TABLE 7-4

Distribution of Sample Units by Stratification
Category and Key Environmental Variables

STRATIFICATION CATEGORY

Distance to Nearest Spring (miles)	Playa Valleys	Other Valleys	Mohave River	Springs	Mountain	Total
=0	0	0	0	7	0	7
0-3.5	2	3	6	0	5	16
3.5-6.5	8	3	7	0	1	19
6.5-9.5	9	7	2	0	0	18
9.5+	13	21	12	0	0	46
Total	32	34	27	7	6	106

Distance to Mojave River (miles)	Playa Valleys	Other Valleys	Mohave River	Springs	Mountain	Total
0-10	3	4	27	1	1	36
10-20	7	14	0	6	5	32
20-30	12	6	0	0	0	18
30-40	7	0	0	0	0	7
40+	3	10	0	0	0	13
Total	32	34	27	7	6	106

TABLE 7-4 (cont.)

	Playa Valleys	Other Valleys	Mojave River	Springs	Mountain	Total
Distance to Nearest Juniper (miles)						
=0	0	0	3	0	5	8
0-5	0	0	0	1	1	2
5-10	3	4	0	0	0	7
10+	29	30	24	6	0	89
Total	32	34	27	7	6	106
Distance to Nearest Playa (miles)						
=0	3	0	0	0	0	3
0-1.5	15	0	0	1	0	16
1.5-3.5	9	2	2	1	0	14
3.5-5.5	4	9	1	3	0	17
5.5+	1	23	24	2	6	56
Total	32	34	27	7	6	106
Yucca/Joshua						
Not present	26	21	15	2	1	65
Present	6	13	12	5	5	41
Total	32	34	27	7	6	106

TABLE 7-4 (cont.)

Elevation (feet)	Playa Valleys	Other Valleys	Mojave River	Springs	Mountain	Total
0-2000	8	6	10	2	0	26
2000-3000	12	11	13	0	0	36
3000-4000	11	17	2	4	1	35
4000-5000	1	0	2	1	2	6
5000+		0	0	0	3	3
Total	32	34	27	7	6	106

Distance to Nearest Mesquite (miles)	Playa Valleys	Other Valleys	Mojave River	Springs	Mountain	Total
=0	2	4	3	3	0	12
0-5	3	6	21	0	1	31
5-10	10	7	3	2	1	23
10+	17	17	0	2	4	40
Total	32	34	27	7	6	106

lute numerical estimates; rather, relative estimates would be the goal. Such estimates may be achieved by comparing different subsets of the total ARID-II sample and asking whether there are statistically significant differences between the subsets in terms of site frequencies or other cultural resource parameters. The importance of statistical significance lies in the fact that one then expects (with a reasonable and measurable degree of certainty) that the differences observed in the sample actually exist throughout the sampling universe. Thus, if the subsets used in the analysis are chosen so that they accurately reflect distinct environmental zones or other meaningful categories, the analysis will lead to useful statements concerning the relative distribution of cultural resources within the area under investigation.

Since the sampling design was developed in large part to facilitate the comparison of different types of valleys, it seemed logical to begin the analysis with such comparisons. The earliest tests concentrate specifically on prehistoric sites.

The first series of tests which were performed were designed to identify any differences between overall site frequencies in sample units lying with the three "Valley" strata: 1) Mojave River Valley, 2) Playa Valleys and 3) Other Valley Types. A variety of different measures of prehistoric sites were used including 1) the mean number of sites per sample unit by block (or cluster; see Chapter 4) and 2) the proportion of sample units which contained (prehistoric) sites by block.

Although these tests did not indicate significant differences between these three valley types, they generally did point toward the conclusion that site frequencies in the Mojave River Valley may be somewhat higher (also see Table 7-1A). This became an important consideration in subsequent tests.

The demonstration of a statistical difference between various groups or categories generally requires high variability (i.e. numerical differences) between categories in relation to the extant variability within categories. In this sense, most statistical tests ask the question, "To what extent has the categorization scheme successfully limited the total observed variation in the topic phenomenon to between- (rather than within-) category differences?" It was felt that these initial tests had failed to indicate differences in site frequencies by valley type due, in large part, to the high degree of variability, in site frequencies, within each valley type. Simply stated, with each stratification category, some blocks had many recorded sites, others had none; within most blocks, some sample units had many sites, others none.

When confronted with this type of problem, it is common to consider whether it is possible to find a controlling variable that will successfully reduce this within-category variation. A reduction in this variation generally indicates that one has moved closer toward a good predictive model and perhaps a better explanatory model as well.

In considering possible controlling variables I immediately turned to an argument that had proven important to the analysis of the Northeast Mojave survey data. The Valley Contour Hypothesis (Coombs 1978) is concerned with the distribution of prehistoric sites across the idealized desert valley in cross-section. In general, the hypothesis argues that, along this cross-section line, sites will tend to predominate at the valley floor and the upper pediment (i.e. the valley/mountain interface).

I felt that there were two basic reasons for expecting to find valley sites concentrated in these ecotonal areas. First, such areas provided more efficient access to a greater number of resources given their position between neighboring resource zones. This argument is consistent with the "site catchment" concept discussed by Thomas and Bettinger (1976: 270), and is perhaps most applicable with respect to sites located along the typical upper pediment. Secondly, I agreed with Vita-Finzi and Higgs (1971) that in some cases sites are found in ecotones because of the primary exploitation of a neighboring zone, which because of its size or other characteristics, is itself uninhabitable (or unexploitable if inhabited). This almost certainly applies to spring locations and mesquite groves, for example. It is also important to stress that I expected lithic as well as biotic resources to have played a role in this site distribution pattern. This is particularly significant along the upper pediment, where detrital outwash activity frequently produces extensive beds of various lithic materials. (Coombs 1978: 91-92)

The statistical techniques that was originally used to test this hypothesis was two-way analysis of variance, employing an approximation method for unequal sub-category frequencies outlined by Walker and Lev (1953: 381-382). In the ARID-I analysis, I categorized each sample unit by valley contour using a simple index: 1) the distance from the sample unit to the valley floor (i.e. the shortest distance to the main valley drainage) <u>divided by</u> 2) the distance from the valley floor to the foot of the mountains located on the same side of the valley as the sample unit itself. This index was thus a means of normalizing data from different valleys; sample units near the valley floor were assigned valley contour values close to zero, units near the mountains received values approximating one, and so on. The analysis was also performed using the following categorization scheme:

1. "Valley Floor" - included sample units assigned valley contour values of 0-0.3 inclusive

2. "Intermediate" - sample units with valley contour ratings be-
    tween 0.3 and 0.7 exclusive

3. "Upper Pediment" - sample units with valley contour values
    from 0.7 to 1.0 inclusive

(The reader should understand that this categorization is different
from the block-location or zone scheme used in Table 7-1A.)

The ARID-II analysis followed these same basic procedures. The
first analysis of variance that was performed contrasted each of
the three valley contour categories and each of the three valley
types ("Playa", "Mojave River", and "Other"). The results did not
indicate significant differences within either of these categorization schemes. In the second test, two categories in each scheme
were combined. First, since the earlier tests had suggested that
more sites may actually exist along the Mojave River Valley, I
combined the "Playa" and "Other Valley" categories to permit a
single comparison. Secondly, since the Valley Contour Hypothesis
predicted higher site frequencies along both the upper pediment
and the valley floor (without quantitatively differentiating
between them), these two categories were also pooled together.
The sampling means and analysis of variance results are shown in
Table 7-5.[1]

Although none of the F-tests presented in Table 7-5 proved
statistically significant, these results did suggest possible
differences that should be explored further. The F-value for
the "interaction" factor (1.73) for example suggested that there
may be a difference between the Mojave River and remaining valley
types, in terms of how sites are distributed across the valley
contour. The resultant means shown in Table 7-5 clarify this
possible difference: the Valley Contour Hypothesis appears to be
supported by the results from the "Playa" and "Other Valley" sample units (i.e. most sites are located at or near the valley floor
or upper pediment) but not by the Mojave River Valley results.

To further test the Valley Contour Hypothesis in the case of
the "non-Mojave" valleys, a t-test was performed (see, for example,
Weinberg and Schumaker 1969: 193-200) which contrasted the site
frequency results from these valleys for the "valley floor/upper
pediment" versus "intermediate" contour categories. The results
proved significant at the 0.05 level. Since there were two large
values in the former category, which may have produced all of the
statistical difference, I also performed a non-parametric alternative to the t-test - Fisher's Exact Test (see Blalock 1960: 221-
225). In this test each sample unit from the "Playa" and "Other"
valleys was categorized by: 1) contour category and 2) whether the
sample unit contained any prehistoric sites. The results, which
are shown in Table 7-6, also proved significant at the 0.05 level.
Quite clearly, in these valley types, and in support of the Valley
Contour Hypothesis, prehistoric sites do tend to be located predominantly within the valley floor and upper pediment regions.

TABLE 7-5

The Distribution of Prehistoric Sites by Valley Contour and Valley Type

ANALYSIS OF VARIANCE

Factor	Sum of Squares	Degrees of Freedom	Estimate of Variance	F-value
Valley Type	1.39	1	1.39	3.76
Contour	0.16	1	0.16	0.44
Interaction	0.63	1	0.63	1.73
Error		64	0.37	

SAMPLE MEANS

	Contour Categories	
Valley Type	Intermediate	Valley Floor and Upper Pediment
Mojave River	2.0	1.61
Playa and Other Valleys	0.03	1.23

TABLE 7-6

The Relationship Between Prehistoric Site Distributions and Valley Contour: Playa and Other Valleys

CONTOUR CATEGORY

	Valley Floor and Upper Pediment	Intermediate	
No sites recorded	24 (70.6)	18 (94.7)	42
Sites recorded	10 (29.4)	1 (5.3)	42
	34	19	53

$p < 0.05$

(Column percentages are shown in parentheses; see note #1 at the end of this chapter for an explanation of marginal totals)

The comparatively high F-value for the "valley-type" factor in Table 7-5 also suggested once again that there exists a difference between the Mojave River and the remaining valley types in terms of prehistoric site densities. To further test this notion, I performed an analysis of variance identical to that described in Table 7-5, except that the upper pediment and valley floor categories were narrowed so that they included the ranges 0.8 to 1.0 and 0 to 0.2, respectively. The results of this test are shown in Table 7-7A. The F-test for the valley-type factor is now significant at the 0.05 level, suggesting the likelihood of a meaningful difference between the Mojave River Valley and "Other Valley" types in the Western Mojave. The non-parametric alternative to this test, consists of a "pooled" Fisher's Exact Test (see Coombs 1978: 82-83). The data for this test are described in Table 7-7B. The pooled probability of these combined results is less than 1 in 100, in further support of a difference between the Mojave River Valley and the other valley types within the project area in terms of the distribution of prehistoric sites.

Let us now concentrate specifically on the Mojave River Valley and consider what may be said concerning this dominant feature of the California Desert.

1. Prehistoric Sites Within the Mojave River Valley

The initial tests described here suggest that the Valley Contour Hypothesis does not apply in the case of the Mojave River Valley. In attempting to understand this discrepancy it is perhaps noteworthy that these earlier tests also indicated the likelihood that there are more prehistoric sites within this valley than in others within the project area. This should not be particularly surprising to most readers, since the Mojave River clearly played a key role in the prehistory of the California Desert as a comparatively reliable provider of water and food resources. Given the importance of the river itself, the simplest and most reasonable alternative to the Valley Contour Hypothesis, and the argument which immediately suggests itself, is that prehistoric site densities are a simple inverse function of the distance to the river - as the distance to the river increases, site densities decline.

To test this alternative expectation, each of the 27 sample units along the Mojave River was categorized with respect to their distance to the river and to the presence/absence of prehistoric sites. The results, shown in Table 7-8A, provide apparent support for the model: as distance to the river increases, the likelihood of finding one or more sites in a particular sample unit tends to decline. Kendall's Tau (a non-parametric correlation technique) for this relationship is -0.54, indicating a comparatively strong association.

There is a problem of interdependence with these results, however, since block membership has not been controlled for.

TABLE 7-7

The Distribution of Prehistoric Sites
by Valley Contour and Valley Type

A. ANALYSIS OF VARIANCE

Factor	Sum of Squares	Degrees of Freedom	Estimate of Variance	F-value
Valley Type	1.43	1	1.43	4.58
Contour	0.17	1	0.17	0.56
Interaction	0.78	1	0.78	2.49
Error		61	0.31	

B. POOLED FISHER'S EXACT TEST

Contour Category

	Valley Floor/Upper Pediment			Intermediate		
	Mojave River Valley	Playa and Other Valleys		Mojave River Valley	Playa and Other Valleys	
No Sites Recorded	3 (0.33)	18 (0.67)	21	2 (0.29)	18 (0.82)	20
Sites Recorded	6 (0.67)	9 (0.33)	15	5 (0.71)	4 (0.18)	9
	9	27	36	7	22	29
		p=0.097			p=0.017	

Pooled probability = 0.002

(Column percentages are shown in parentheses: see note #1 at the end of this chapter for an explanation of marginal totals)

Such controls can be implemented simply by insuring that each sample unit from a given block falls into a separate category. The ARID-II sampling design is well equipped to handle this problem since the sample units within each block begin at the valley floor and extend upward across one side of the valley; thus, within a given block, it is possible to place each transect in a "block location" category: "close" (i.e. closest to the valley floor), "intermediate" and "far" (This corresponds to the "zone" categorization scheme used in Table 7-1A).

By transforming the results from Table 7-8A to accomodate this new categorization scheme, the figures shown in Table 7-8B are obtained. As before, the results support the argument that sites tend to cluster around the river and decline in numbers as distance to the river increases. Kendall's Tau for this view of the relationship is -0.4, which is statistically significant at the 0.05 level (z = -1.88).

The reader should understand that these results do not imply that site frequencies are highest near the river. Rather and more precisely, they indicate that the likelihood of finding some prehistoric sites is greatest in the immediate vicinity of the river. In fact, more prehistoric sites were recorded in the two outer block locations than in that closest to the river! These apparently contradictory facts are easily reconciled once it is understood that although the outer sample units were less likely to have sites, those that did, often had very many.

In combination, these various facts regarding the Mojave River Valley sub-sample led to the generation of the following set of arguments and predictions:

a. The Mojave River was a prime resource area. Thus at virtually any location along its course, there is a very high probability of finding prehistoric sites associated with the exploitation of riverine resources (among other things, this may account for the comparatively low variability in site frequencies per sample unit within the immediate vicinity of the river; see Table 7-1A). Similarly, as one moves further from the river, the probability of finding such special purpose sites should decline.

b. Habitation sites, in contrast to exploitative or extractive sites, are less likely perhaps to be found in direct association with the river for two basic reasons:

1) Generally speaking, food production/collection cannot be effectively practiced within the confines of a habitation area. In the case of hunting, in particular, the most productive strategy would usually demand habitation some distance removed from the primary hunting area.

TABLE 7-8

The Effect of the Mojave River on the
Distribution of Prehistoric Sites

A. DISTANCE TO THE MOJAVE RIVER

Distance (miles)

	0-1	1-2	2-3	3+
No Sites Recorded	3 (0.23)	5 (0.62)	4 (0.8)	1 (1.0)
Sites Recorded	10 (0.77)	3 (0.38)	1 (0.2)	0 (0)
Proportion of Sample Units with Sites	0.77	0.38	0.2	0.0

B. BLOCK LOCATION

	Close (zone 1)	Intermediate (zone 2)	Far (zone 3)
No Sites Recorded	2 (0.22)	5 (0.56)	6 (0.67)
Sites Recorded	7 (0.78)	4 (0.44)	3 (0.33)
Proportion of Sample Units with Sites	0.78	0.44	0.33

(Column percentages are shown in parentheses)

2) River action itself, particularly periodic flooding, would preclude habitation of any duration in the immediate vicinity of the river.

Together, the arguments suggest that habitation sites, in particular, may tend to predominate at a distance from the river.

c. Unlike the specialized extractive site, habitation sites require a _variety_ of resources and other local conditions to make them practical and liveable. Thus, I expected habitation sites to be much more localized (or clustered). This, I thought, could conceivably account for the higher observed variability in site densities at greater distances from the river.

As support for these arguments, I needed to first demonstrate that habitation sites tended to predominate among the _outlying_ sites along the river. This, in fact, proved to be the case. Of the nine prehistoric sites recorded during the Mojave River Valley portion of the inventory which were classified as habitation sites (i.e. temporary camps or villages; see Appendix I) only one was found in the "close" block location; all others were found in the sample units in the "intermediate" category (see Table 7-9A). Using a Fisher's Exact Test (and pooling the "close" and "far" block location results), I found that the probability of finding 89% (8 of 9) of all recorded habitation sites in the "intermediate" block location was less than 0.02. This appeared a rather good indication that, in the Mojave River Valley, habitation sites are not randomly distributed with respect to other, special activity sites, but actually tend to occur at a rather predictable distance from the river. In fact, all of the habitation sites proved to fall within a comparatively restricted outlying zone - between 0.6 and 1.0 miles from the river. This rather striking pattern is shown in Table 7-9B.

Several comments are in order regarding the above findings. First, it should be pointed out that none of the habitation sites recorded during the inventory were large permanent midden sites. All were categorized as temporary camps rather than villages, and this classification was based on the variety of artifacts and features observed at each site (see Appendix I). Secondly, it is noteworthy that, at other locations along the Mojave River, large village sites with considerable cultural deposition have been recorded (see Rector n.d. and Smith 1963). Typically, these village sites are found immediately adjacent to the river (It is noteworthy, in terms of an earlier argument, that these sites exhibit evidence of periodic flooding) and may be limited, for the most part to the zone extending between _____ and _____. For the most part, this zone was not available for survey due to the extensive pattern of private land ownership there. Thus it appears likely that the site distrib-

TABLE 7-9

The Distribution of Habitation and
Special Activity Sites in Relation to the Mojave River

A. BLOCK LOCATION

	Close (zone 1)	Intermediate (zone 2)	Far (zone 3)
Total Habitation Sites Recorded	1 (0.11)	8 (0.89)	0 (0)
Total Special Activity Sites Recorded	11 (0.27)	17 (0.41)	13 (0.32)

B. DISTANCE TO THE MOJAVE RIVER

Distance (miles)

	0-0.6	0.6-1.0	1.0+
Total Habitation Sites Recorded	0 (0)	9 (1.0)	0 (0)
Total Special Activity Sites Recorded	11 (0.27)	16 (0.39)	14 (0.34)

(Row percentages are shown in parentheses)

ution patterns described above may apply uniquely to that portion of the river included in the ARID-II Inventory and that very different patterns exist elsewhere along the river. Eric Ritter (personal communication) has suggested that this difference may reflect concommitant differences in environmental diversity.

I wished also to try and show that the special activity sites that we recorded were, in fact, associated with the habitation sites. Basically, it was expected that this association would manifest itself in the form of specialized sites clustering around habitation sites, reflecting the "base camp" function of the habitation area. This notion was tested in a simple fashion, using analysis of covariance and comparing site frequencies per sample unit from the "close" and "far" block locations, respectively, with those from the "intermediate" category (the "independent variable"). The results, which are shown in Table 7-10, indicate a rather strong relationship. Thus it would appear that special activity sites do cluster and increase in number in association with habitation areas. In a causal sense, however, this does not mean, of course, that the selection of a habitation site determined the area of specialized activity; far more likely, of course, the resource potential of different areas influenced the ultimate selection of a habitation site.

It should be clear to the reader that, with regard to this last argument, no evidence has been provided in support of the contemporaneity of sites. This does not overly concern me, however. I would expect to find, with a complete record of prehistoric activity, essentially the same locational patterns, at isolated points in time, that have been described here. The fact that we have been able to see these patterns at all, with a compressed and only partially intact record, may indicate that the same Mojave River locations were employed again and again, over a long period of time, as principal settlement/subsistence areas.

It should be mentioned that the erosion patterns that characterize the Mojave River region may have artificially created the prehistoric site patterns described above. Specifically, there may have been relatively more sites closer to the river than these results suggest. Again, however, one would not expect a more complete record to discount the relationships identified here, although additional relationships might then emerge.

At this point in the analysis, and as a means of reaffirming the quantitative findings, I took a more detailed, qualitative look at the map locations of the ARID-II sites along the Mojave. As expected, most sites were located along the edges of terraces adjacent to and above the river. The habitation sites, in particular, tended to predominate here. The map

TABLE 7-10

Site Clustering Along the Mojave River

ANALYSIS OF COVARIANCE RESULTS

Y-variates: Prehistoric Sites per Sample Unit, "close" and "far" block locations.

X-variates: Prehistoric Sites per Sample Unit, "intermediate" block location.

Y-variate	Slope	r^2
"close"	+0.24	0.58
"far"	+0.53	0.63
Total	+0.38	0.54

TEST FOR SIGNIFICANCE OF AVERAGE WITHIN-CLASS CORRELATION

$$F_{1,15} = 17.91 \qquad p < 0.001$$

investigation provided little insight to the observed variability in site frequencies between sampled blocks. River
vegetation, for example, did not appear at all useful (a conclusion further supported by quantitative analyses not described here). All blocks which contained large numbers of
sites were found to be located on the north side of the
river, between _____ and _____. No other patterns were observed.

In conclusion, the following generalizations appear to
apply to the distribution of prehistoric sites along the
Mojave River:

a. The likelihood of finding sites tends to decline as the
    distance to the river increases.

b. Habitation sites tend to occur at a more or less fixed
    distance from the river, perhaps between 0.6 and 1.0 miles.

c. Special activity sites tend to cluster around habitational
    sites; as the latter increase in number, so do the former.

It is important to point out once again, however, that the
Mojave River Valley sample necessarily excluded private lands
and that there is good reason to believe that site distribution
patterns on these lands might be quite different. Let us now
return to an evaluation of the remaining valley types.

2. Prehistoric Sites in the Playa and Other Valleys

The relationship between prehistoric site locations and
valley contour, in the case of the "Playa" and "Other" valley
types, is perhaps most evident if block membership is ignored
for the moment and each sample unit is categorized by a) contour category and b) whether or not any prehistoric sites were
recorded. The individual and combined results for these two
valley types are shown in Table 7-11. The table indicates a
rather strong tendency for sites to be located in the extreme
contour categories. In total, only 5% (1 of 20) of the sample
units located in the intermediate contour category contained
prehistoric sites; over 29% of the transects in each of the
remaining categories contained sites (it is perhaps noteworthy
that appropriate adjustments of the contour category limits
resulted in an even stronger depiction of this relationship).

At this point in the analysis regression and correlation
were employed. Since the Valley Contour Hypothesis does not
differentiate between valley floor and upper pediment areas,
in the sense that high relative site frequencies are predicted
for each, I decided it would be possible to employ regression
by first "folding" the valley contour variable. Mechanically,
this involved subtracting the valley contour value for a given

TABLE 7-11

The Distribution of Prehistoric Sites
by Valley Contour: Playa and Other Valleys

CONTOUR CATEGORY

		0-0.3	0.3-0.7	0.7-1.0
A.	PLAYA VALLEYS			
	No Sites Recorded	9 (64.3)	9 (100.00)	7 (77.8)
	Sites Recorded	5 (35.7)	0 (0)	2 (22.2)
B.	OTHER VALLEYS			
	No Sites Recorded	6 (75.0)	10 (90.9)	10 (66.7)
	Sites Recorded	2 (25.0)	1 (9.1)	5 (33.3)
C.	PLAYA AND OTHER VALLEYS COMBINED			
	Sites Recorded	17 (70.8)	19 (95.0)	17 (70.8)
	Sites Recorded	7 (29.2)	1 (5.0)	7 (29.2)

(Column percentages are shown in parentheses)

TABLE 7-12

The Effect of Valley Width on
Prehistoric Site Distributions

VALLEY WIDTH

		≤ 3	>3	
A.	PLAYA AND OTHER VALLEYS			
	No Sites Recorded in Block	1 (16.7)	13 (72.2)	$p < 0.05$
	Sites Recorded in Block	5 (83.3)	5 (27.8)	
B.	ALL BLOCKS			
	No Sites Recorded in Block	2 (22.2)	18 (75.0)	$p < 0.01$
	Sites Recorded in Block	7 (77.8)	6 (25.0)	

(Column percentages are shown in parentheses)

transect from 1, if that value exceeded 0.5. In essence, this new measure provides the distance from a particular sample unit to either the valley floor or the upper pediment, which-ever is closest, expressed as a proportion of the overall valley width. The value of this measure, of course, is that the valley contour argument predicts that sites will tend to cluster in the neighborhood of the zero value. Moreover, this measure permitted the use of regression and correlation as a means of determining if site densities actually did tend to decline (thus far the analysis has simply dichotomized between tran-sects with and those without sites) as sample units fell further and further away from the valley floor or upper pediment.

In the first regression, all sample unit results from the "Playa" and "Other" valley sampling categories were included. The resulting Pearson correlation, -0.35, proved significant at the 0.01 level in an F-test. This seemed a good indication of the predictive accuracy of the Valley Contour Hypothesis. This first test, however, did not include any controls for variations from one valley (i.e. sampling block) to another in terms of overall site densities. It should be clear to the reader that such variations are irrelevant to the valley contour argument, since it is concerned only with the rela-tive distribution of sites across a given valley. A simple way to implement this type of control is to delete all blocks in which no sites were recorded (it should be understood that this segment of the sample tells us absolutely nothing one way or the other, about the validity of the Valley Contour Hypothesis). Having made these deletions, the regression was performed once again. The results, which are shown in Figure 7-1, indicate a rather strong relationship between site density and valley contour.

An examination of Figure 7-1 reveals that the distribution of points tends to form a rough triangle. I have attempted to define this triangle with a series of parallel lines running between the X and Y axes. When the relationship between two variables describes this type of triangle, it is often an indication that one or more confounding variables are dis-guising an even stronger relationship. We might consider the imposed lines in the figure as a graphic control over these unknown, exogenous variables. If we were to superimpose the lines, bringing with each line the points nearest to it, a quite strong inverse linear relationship between the variables would graphically emerge. My task, then, became one of attempt-ing to analytically replicate this graphic superimposition.

The first effort in this direction involved using Analysis of Covariance and differentiating by block. In essence, this consisted of testing to see to what extent differences between blocks could account for the discrepancies observed in Figure 7-1.[4] The results were quite encouraging; the Pearson Corre-lation (i.e. the average within-block correlation) was lifted

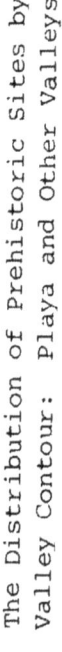

FIGURE 7-1

The Distribution of Prehistoric Sites by
Valley Contour: Playa and Other Valleys

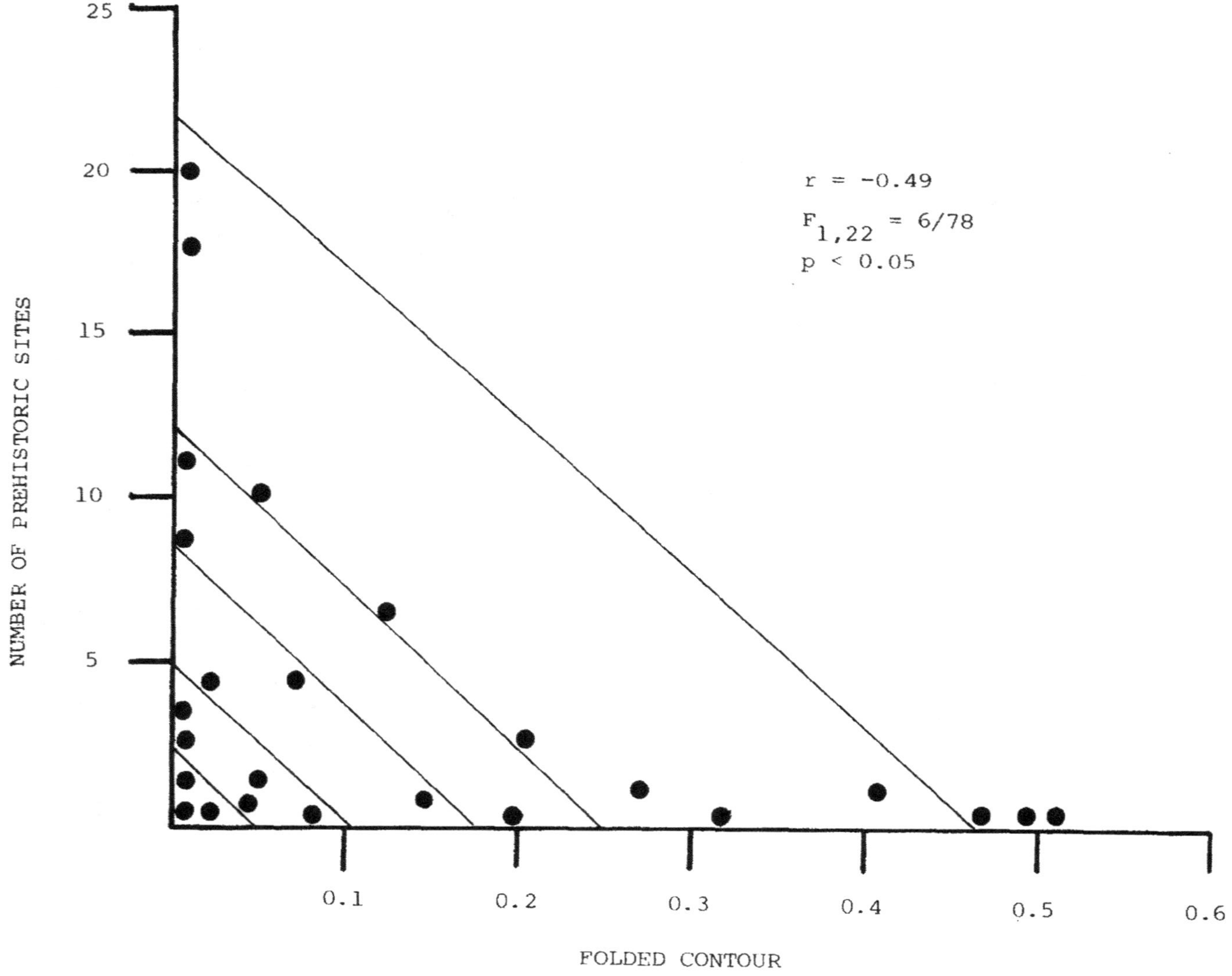

r = -0.49

$F_{1,22}$ = 6/78

p < 0.05

FOLDED CONTOUR

NUMBER OF PREHISTORIC SITES

to -0.6 and the testing revealed homogeneity of slopes and no interaction. In short, this indicated that the valley contour argument was supported by results from the average block, that the form that the relationship takes was comparatively constant from one block to the next, and that the differences from block to block in terms of overall site density were disguising a stronger relationship between site distribution patterns and valley contour.

Controlling for block, of course, entirely avoids the question of why differences exist between blocks. I realized that if I could develop a model to account for inter-block variability, then this model, when coupled with the valley contour argument, would provide a very meaningful package for predicting prehistoric site distributions.

The reader will recall that the Valley Contour Hypothesis is based on existing arguments concerning the importance of ecotones or similar zones which provide close access to a variety of critical resources. A complementary hypothesis derived from this latter argument (and thus a test implication for it) involves a possible inverse relationship between site frequencies and valley width. According to this argument, narrow valleys are like macro-ecotones in the sense that they provide a variety of resources in a comparatively compact area. Accordingly, I expected to find an association between site frequencies and valley width.

Table 7-12A shows the result when blocks from the "Playa" and "Other" valley sampling strata are categorized by valley width (a width of three miles was selected as the category boundary) and the presence/absence of prehistoric sites. The tendency for sites to predominate in the narrower valleys is quite evident: over 80% of the blocks located in narrow valleys contained sites; less than 30% of those in the wide valleys had sites. Results from the Mojave River Valley also follow this general pattern. The results when the Mojave River blocks are included is shown in Table 7-12B. Both sets of results are significant at the 0.05 level in a Fisher's Exact Test, a good indication of the relationship between valley width and site distributions between valleys.[3]

Quite by accident, I discovered what may prove to be an equally important predictor of inter-valley site variability. I had been using multiple-regression analysis as a simple means of trying to develop an accurate, if theoretically "dumb", model for predicting site distribution patterns. I was quite surprised to find that the distance to the Mojave River continued to crop up as an important predictor variable. Obviously there are good reasons for expecting the location of the river to have a significant impact on site distributions. What was surprising, however, was that this influence appeared to extend for a considerable distance, well beyond the Mojave River Valley itself, for example. This is shown in Table 7-13A, in which blocks are categorized by the mean distance to the river. When these results are coupled with the earlier finding that sample units along the river itself have the highest average site frequencies of all (see above), it becomes clear that there is a very good case for the argument that the Mojave River played a truly dominant role in the prehistory of the Western Mojave Desert.

A simple test of the combined influence of these two factors - valley width and distance to the Mojave - was then attempted. This involved taking the width and river distance figures for each block, multiplying them together and categorizing as before. The rather striking results are described in Table 7-13B. Thus, it would appear that these two factors can potentially account for much of the inter-valley variability observed in the prehistoric site distributions. When this is coupled with the findings concerning the relationship between valley contour and intra-valley variability, it becomes clear that considerable progress has been made here toward accounting for much of the total variability present in prehistoric site distribution patterns in the Western Mojave.

3. Prehistoric Sites in Mountain Locations

The Research Design Conference which laid the groundwork for the ARID-II Sampling Design, elected to place mountain transects exclusively in the ranges lying along the southwestern border of the project area. These ranges were selected for prime consideration because they seemed to differ in a variety of ways from other desert ranges, perhaps most notably in terms of their comparative accessibility to coastal populations, and their relatively weak association with the characteristic desert environment.

Other ranges in the Western Mojave were excluded from consideration (with the exception of spring-oriented sample units) because we felt there was a strong likelihood that these did not differ significantly from those in other areas in terms of cultural resources, and more importantly because the ARID-II sample size seemed to preclude even a testing of this assumption.

Given this background to the selection of mountain transects, it seemed appropriate to compare the results from ARID-I and ARID-II. The ARID-I sample included 40 randomly-placed mountain transects; 4 (10%) of these contained prehistoric sites. ARID-II included 6 mountain transects and prehistoric sites were recorded in 2 (33%) of these. In spite of the small sample sizes, a Fisher's Exact Test indicated a meaningful difference between these results: the "hit" density of sample units in the southwestern ranges of the Western Mojave proved to be significantly higher at the 0.01 confidence level.

TABLE 7-13A

The Effect of the Mojave River on Prehistoric
Site Distributions: Playa and Other Valleys

DISTANCE TO THE MOHAVE RIVER

	$\leq$ 30 miles	>30 miles
No Sites Recorded in Block	8 (47.1)	6 (85.7)
Sites Recorded	9 (52.9)	1 (14.3)

p= 0.097

(Column percentages are shown in parentheses)

TABLE 7-13B

The Effect of Valley Width and Distance to the Mojave
River on Prehistoric Site Distributions: Playa and Other Valleys

INDEX: VALLEY WIDTH x DISTANCE TO RIVER

	0-50 miles	50-100 miles	100+ miles
No Sites Recorded in Block	1 (16.7)	2 (40.0)	11 (84.6)
Sites Recorded	5 (83.3)	3 (60.0)	2 (15.4)

Kendall's Tau = -0.62
z = -2.9
p < 0.01

(Column percentages are shown in parentheses)

Thus, to the extent that the Northeastern Mojave may be considered representative of the California Desert in general, these results support our assumption concerning the relative archaeological potential of the boundary mountains of the Western Mojave (nevertheless, no archaeological evidence pointing specifically to seasonal occupation or other uses by coastal groups was recorded during the fieldwork). Hopefully, this testing may be further pursued, by including results from other desert areas.

4. Springs and the Distribution of Sites

In the analysis of the Northeast Mojave data, an attempt was made to show that cultural resource sites, both historic and prehistoric, tend to be associated with springs; that is, all other things being equal, a given site is more likely to be found close to a spring than far away. This basic pattern also may be demonstrated for the Western Mojave Desert.

Consider Table 7-14A, which involves data from the valley-block sub-sample. In the table, each block is categorized by a) the mean distance of sample units in the block to the nearest recorded spring and b) whether any prehistoric sites were recorded with the block. These results, which indicate a clear tendency for blocks containing prehistoric sites to be located near springs, are statistically significant (in a Fisher's Exact Test) at the 0.05 level. Consider also Table 7-14B. Here, the previous categorization scheme has been broken up by valley-type. For each valley-type, the proportion of "hits" (sample units with sites) is highest for blocks lying within six miles of a spring. The pooled probability of this result is less than 1 in 30. These data thus suggest that, at least on a macroscopic level (i.e. using a comparatively long-distance categorization scheme), [prehistoric sites tend to cluster in the neighborhood of springs, regardless of the type of valley involved.] These results, when coupled with analogous ones from the Northeast Mojave analysis, suggest the likelihood of a desert-wide phenomenon.

These findings, however, tell us absolutely nothing about the effect of springs on a microscopic level - within a one-mile radius, for example. The spring-oriented portion of the ARID-II sample was designed specifically to deal with this very question. Before examining the results from this sub-sample, I would like to outline the argument which I believed might account for the distribution of prehistoric sites in the immediate vicinity of springs.

I felt that within a comparatively close radius, perhaps a mile or so, the spring was a dominating force. Within this relatively restricted zone, one can think of the spring as a target, in the sense that all prehistoric activity was in some sense oriented in relation to the spring. A variety of activi-

TABLE 7-14

The Effect of Spring Locations on the Distribution
of Prehistoric Sites: Valley-Block Sub-Sample

A.   ALL VALLEY-BLOCKS TOGETHER

Mean Distance to Nearest Recorded Spring

	≤ 6 miles	>6 miles
No Sites Recorded in Block	2 (0.2)	14 (0.6)
Sites Recorded in Block	8 (0.8)	9 (0.4)

p = 0.0375

B.   CONTROLLING FOR VALLEY TYPE

	Playa Valleys		Mojave River Valley		Other Valleys	

Mean Distance to Nearest Recorded Spring

	$\leq$ =6	>6	$\leq$ =6	>6	$\leq$ =6	>6
No Sites Recorded in Block	1 (0.2)	6 (0.8)	1 (0.5)	6 (0.6)	0 (0)	2 (0.4)
Sites Recorded in Block	3 (0.8)	2 (0.2)	1 (0.5)	4 (0.9)	4 (1)	3 (0.6)

p = 0.15   p = 0.68   p = 0.20

pooled probability = 0.029

(Column percentages are shown in parentheses)

ties would be involved here including hunting, collecting, camping, watering and so on. Of course, not all of these would occur precisely at the spring; but all would be heavily influenced by the spring and its often dramatic impact on other local resources. Thus we might reasonably expect to find the evidence of these activites distributed around the spring, that is, with the spring serving as the distribution's center. Weinberg and Schumaker (1969: 113-114) have described, in very understandable terms, how the orientation of behavior in relation to a particular target can result in a normal dis-tribution of behavior around that target. Because it seemed reasonable to think of the spring as a behavioral target, I anticipated finding prehistoric sites normally distributed around spring locations.

An effort was made to test this argument using the spring-oriented sub-sample. The reader will recall that this portion of the sample consisted of seven transects placed across a random sample of recorded springs. Each of these units was graphically divided width-wise into two parts, each part extend-ing outward from the spring.[4] All of these various sample unit segments were then pooled together in order to determine how much area had been inventoried within various zones surround-ing the springs in the sample. Next, for each recorded site, the distance to the appropriate spring was determined. Finally, the site and area figures were used to estimate prehistoric site densities at different distances from the springs. The findings are shown in Table 7-15. These results suggest that sites do cluster most densely immediately surrounding the springs and that site density declines as distance to the spring increases. There is at least a rough approximation of a normal distribution, although there are very few data here to allow very meaningful testing. Similarly, the differences recorded in Table 7-15 do not prove to be statistically signifi-cant. Nevertheless, I think it is appropriate to say that the argument presented here has received some valid support and thus should be tested further.

The spring transects are also noteworthy for the diversity of prehistoric activities represented archaeologically. Of the two recorded sites containing pottery, one is located in a spring transect. Similarly, 40% (2 of 5) of the sites con-taining grinding implements and one of the four recorded pro-jectile points were found in these sample units. These results become particularly meaningful when one recognizes that the spring sub-sample represents only 6.6% (7 of 106 transects) of the total area covered during the ARID-II fieldwork.

Since only seven historic sites were recorded during the inventory, comparatively little can be generalized concerning historic sites in the Western Mojave. One of the few conclu-sions that can be tentatively reached involves spring locations and their apparent affect on the distribution of historic sites

TABLE 7-15

The Effect of Spring Locations on the Distribution
of Prehistoric Sites: Spring Sub-Sample

Zone (Distance to spring in miles)	0-0.05	0.05-0.25	0.25-1.0
Total Sites Recorded	2	3	1
Area Inventoried (sq. miles)	0.08	0.30	0.49
Site Density Estimate (sites/sq. miles)	25	10	2

Three of the seven recorded historic sites were found in spring transects. Again, this suggests a rather strong association between historic activity in the desert and spring locations. Controlling for site type, this relationship appears even stronger; three of the four recorded historic sites which are not related to mining were located in spring transects. Even if blocks are treated as single observations (that is, equivalent to single transects),[5] both versions of this relationship prove statistically significant in a Fisher's Exact Test. Clearly, springs have played a major role in the spatial patterning of human activity through many phases of the desert's occupation.

5. Historic Sites Related to Mining

The recorded sites related to historic mining do not exhibit the striking relationship with spring locations which appears in the case of other historic site types. Rather, these three mining-related sites are distributed in a different but equally understandable pattern: one is located in a mountain transect, a second was found in the mountainous portion of a "Valley" transect, and the third is located in the heart of the Gold-stone Mining District. These results agree rather well with the findings from the Northeast Mojave, which place mines and other sites related to mining in mountain/pediment areas or other prime resource zones.

E. Summary and Conclusions

This chapter has been addressed to the analytical results and conclusions derived from ARID-II. The presentation has included only a small number of "independent" variables. Specifically, I have stressed the importance of the Mojave River, spring locations, valley width, and contour at one or more places in the discussion. Other variables, most notably those involving vegetation, were included in the analysis but did not prove significant predictors of site patterning. To a certain extent, perhaps, this may be attibuted to the small size of the ARID-II sample. It is also possible that the validity problem associated with the measurement of vegetation and other comparatively transient desert phenomena (see Chapter 6) is partially responsible for this result. Nevertheless, I would hope that the few environmental factorswhich have been stressed here can provide valuable insights to the distribution of prehistoric and historic resources not only in the Western Mojave but in other California Desert areas as well.

NOTES

1. To avoid possible biases created by the block/cluster sampling technique, sample unit results were combined whenever two or more sample units from the same block also fell in the same contour category. For the Analyses of Variance, this was accomplished by using the mean number of sites per sample unit, for all sample units involved; in the case of the non-parametric tests, the multiple sample units were treated as a single sample unit.

2. To perform this test, I needed to delete three additional cases - those blocks in which there was no variation from transect to transect in terms of folded contour value.

3. I want to point out that I am less confident of the meaningfulness of this relationship than of others described in this chapter. Basically, my skepticism stems from the realization that many important variables undoubtedly covary with valley width. This is not to say that valley width is a poor predictor, simply that it may not be theoretically relevant.

4. For example, if the spring in a given transect was located 3/10 of a mile from one end of the unit, the resulting parts would be 3/10 and 7/10 miles long, respectively.

5. This treatment permits us to avoid the interdependence of sample units within blocks.

CHAPTER 8. EVALUATIONS AND RECOMMENDATIONS

The primary purpose of this report is to provide input relevant to the management and protection of the cultural resources in the Western Mojave Desert. Toward this end, the present chapter will be used to briefly summarize the major findings of the research regarding the distribution of sites in this portion of the desert and to present some suggestions and ideas which should be useful in making planning decisions.

A. Working Assumptions

In the process of preparing the recommendations presented here, a series of guiding assumptions were developed. These include both facts and subjective impressions concerning the manifold problems that confront the cultural resource manager. In the hope that these assumptions themselves may assist some readers in making management decisions, or in developing alternative suggestions, I will briefly itemize them:

1. Practically speaking, it is impossible to protect all cultural resources in an area as large as the Western Mojave. If it were possible, the ARID-II inventory would be largely unnecessary.

2. There are, however, many different ways in which cultural resources may be protected, or their information preserved.

3. The collections of relevant historical, cultural and other information regarding a particular site, through written records, photography and other means, may be, in many cases, an adequate alternative to the preservation of the site materials themselves. For comparatively simple sites, for example, this may prove sufficient from a research standpoint, although other possible uses of the site (e.g. its religious significance) also should be considered.

4. Management decisions should be designed to help insure that at least one of these preservation measures is applied to all cultural resources in the area involved.

5. Decisions regarding the relative fates of different cultural resources should be based on their comparative value or significance.

6. Many types of significance may be identified, including:

    a. significance to theoretical or historical research;

    b. value to education;

    c. religious, sentimental or aesthetic value intrinsic or
        attached to the resources themselves; and

    d. monetary or exchange value (this last is included because
        it is an important factor in the differential looting of
        sites).

7. With the exception of the last, all of these forms of signif-
    icance are fundamentally harmonious; while the resulting pri-
    orities may be frequently quite different, each is ultimately
    concerned, either directly or indirectly, with the preservation
    and documentation of the cultural past. This, then, is the
    unifying significance theme.

8. Management decisions should take into consideration the fact
    that value systems do change; what is not valued today, may
    be valued in the future (and vice-versa). This potentially
    applies to all of the significance types identified above.

B. Recommendations

    My primary recommendation, and it is an important one, is that
evaluations and preservation measures should be applied whenever
possible to areas rather than isolated sites. Even when a situation
necessitates focus upon a particularly significant site, I would
recommend efforts toward including it in a larger focal area.
Ideally, such areas should be set aside as cultural resource preserves (it may be necessary or desirable to coordinate the selection
of these preserves with other environmentalists who may also wish
to identify preservation areas).

    This emphasis on areas is derived, for the most part, from the
fact that sites, like so many phenomenon, are understandable only
in the context in which they occur. The socio-cultural as well as
the natural environment are involved here. Without a regional context, it becomes difficult if not impossible to determine, for
example, prehistoric settlement and subsistence patterns (much the
same can be said for historic activity in the desert). These patterns of occupation, exploration, subsistence and extraction should
serve as the basic building blocks in the reconstruction of the
history of human occupation in the Desert. Without these regional
building blocks, we are left with a predominantly disjointed collection of facts.

    Since the emphasis on resource areas is born of an interest in
site patterning and diversity within areas, it is important that
the areas be larger than some minimum size (personally, I would
like to see a one square mile minimum, although I have no explicit
rationale for setting this particular limit). For this same reason,
it is recommended that measures be taken to insure that resource
areas vary in shape and run across environmental zones (if there

is an anthropological fact, it is that cultural diversity occurs across environments).

The ARID-II sampling design and analysis have not been designed to determine the relative cultural resource potentials for major regions within the Western Mojave. Rather, they have been developed to identify environments, many of which crosscut geographical and cultural regions, in which cultural resource sites tend to be found. Without detailing the specific results of the analysis, the following general patterns have been observed:

1. The analysis has pointed toward two environmental zones, one stretching along the Mojave River and the other surrounding springs, which appear to have the greatest site density, diversity and complexity within the project area. Previous investigations (see Chapter 3 above) also have emphasized the importance of the Mojave River region, including Manix Basin, in both the prehistory and history of the study area.

2. Less spectacularly, site densities appear to be higher in narrow valleys and valleys proximate to the Mojave River.

3. Within valleys (with the notable exception of the Mojave River Valley) sites seem to cluster along the valley floor and upper pediment.

I recommend that resource areas be selected so as to include a disproportionately large areal sample of these environmental categories emphasized in the analysis. Among other considerations, this will help ensure that preservation areas are allocated in an efficient and effective manner with respect to cultural resources. The preservation areas should include more than simply these focal zones, however, since areas with low site densities (as well as those without sites) can contribute substantially to our understanding of the desert's cultural past.

Additionally, there are a number of important sites, site complexes, or resource areas, which were known to exist prior to the initiation of the ARID-II research. Many of these are identified in Chapter 3. These sites and resource zones should also be given consideration in the development of preservation areas.

Finally, it is crucial that the set of preservation areas that are established does not consist exclusively of areas that have been at least partially inventoried. Areas in the Western Mojave not covered in this or earlier surveys also contain sites, of course, and it would be a grave error to permit a series of random (and/or judgemental) sampling procedures to play a dominant role in the selection of preservation zones. It is recommended that the determination of preservation areas within these uninventoried domains be based largely on the criteria identified above.

To this point, I have made no suggestions as to what should be done within any preservation areas that may be eventually selected. To a large extent, this must be dependent upon what is and will be happening to the Desert and its cultural resources. In this regard, it is absolutely crucial to emphasize that the Western Mojave stands in sharp contrast with most other California Desert areas in terms of on-going and projected developments and other adverse impacts. This is primarily a result of the Western Mojave's relative proximity to the metropolitan areas of the Southern California coast.

Given the comparatively extensive, and frequently destructive, uses of the Western Mojave, it is strongly recommended that immediate action be taken in this area. Some localities should be inventoried without further delay. Areas adjoining the major population centers of the Western Mojave and those favored in recreational pursuits (e.g. playas and analagous areas used for off-road vehicles) should receive high priority here. It may prove desirable to collect isolates and perhaps other small sites to avoid their loss to looters.

Efforts also should be taken to protect sites and resource areas as best as possible. This may involve fencing or added patrolling for especially vulnerable areas. For some types of sites, documentation by means of interpretive signs may provide protection and permit constructive use as well. Regardless of the measures taken, time is of the essence. There is an urgency for protection in the Western Mojave which is unmatched perhaps in the California Desert.

C. Site Evaluation

In the ARID-I report, a series of criteria were developed and used to evaluate, along a series of dimensions, the sites recorded during the ARID-I fieldwork. A subset of these criteria are employed here.

1. Functional Types and Significance

Although some sites may provide quantitatively more information about the past than certain others, each can provide its own unique insights. In general, I am convinced that each class of sites, even the simplest, is indispensable to a thorough understanding of the prehistory and history of the desert. It would be foolish, for example, to decide to preserve all prehistoric villages or all mines at the expense of other types. Accordingly, no ranking of specific functional site types, on the basis of adjudged significance, is attempted here. Rather, other differentiating criteria are applied.

2. Accessibility

In the Western Mojave, as in other desert regions, it is common to find that those sites which exhibit the greatest degree of vandalism are also those which are most accessible from existing towns, roads and trails. Comparatively inaccessible sites, especially those in some mountainous areas, have been afforded a degree of natural protection which lessens the need for imposed protection. Thus, accessibility should be an important consideration in the selection of preservation areas and in the allocation of protective measures. Sites located especially near contemporary towns and roadways are therefore distinguished in the site evaluation (Appendix V, unpublished).

3. Familiarity and Value

It is evident that the vandalism and looting of sites go hand in hand with the familiarity of the resources and their value to the transgressor. Flake scatters, for example, are probably seldom looted, partly because they are not easily recognized as sites and partly because waste flakes and cores are not cherished as much as projectile points or other well-formed tools. Once again, the criteria of familiarity and value are important because they provide an insight to the relative likelihood that a particular site will be disrupted or destroyed.

4. Complexity-Delicacy

Sites that are organizationally complex (e.g. midden sites) are also generally quite delicate in the sense that the information which they contain is relatively vulnerable to destruction, whether by human or natural agents. The site evaluation thus distinguishes those sites determined to be particularly complex and/or delicate.

5. Preservation Requirements

The differentiation of sites on the basis of relative complexity/delicacy is especially germane because the resulting classes of sites demand different preservation/mitigation measures. As organizationally-simple sites, isolated artifacts, for example, are comparatively easy to collect and place in museum collections, little information is generally lost in this process, and henceforth the artifacts remain secure from looters.

Our Native American consultants all felt that authorized collection and museum curation of artifacts was a necessary evil in light of the extensiveness of site destruction in the desert. Although other Native Californians clearly disagree with this position, I definitely side with our consultants and hope that the BLM will carefully consider the possibility of limited collecting in future desert inventories.

The most complex sites (e.g. multi-component occupation areas) are not easily collected, considerable information is usually lost, and there is a high risk of violating burial or other sacred locations. These are the sites that should be left intact and which should be emphasized in the allocation of _in situ_ protection and preservation efforts.

In the case of some sites, the recovery of information essential to research and education does not require the collection of materials or destructive measures. Photography, mapping and other unobtrusive recording may successfully preserve the bulk of information from sites of intermediate complexity, such as flake scatters or rock art.

Since different types of sites are best dealt with using divergent protection/preservation techniques, an effort has been made in the site evaluation to categorize cultural resources on the basis of their relative preservation needs.

6. Mode of Destruction

Finally, sites judged to be particularly endangered were classified on the basis of the type of destruction involved. The following categories were applied:

a. Construction or other recent human activity that is not intentionally destructive

b. Deterioration (applicable to historic structures and rock art, for example)

c. Vandalism

d. Erosion

The results of the site evaluation are reported in Appendix V (unpublished).

C. Conclusions

The development of recommendations for the protection of cultural resources in the Western Mojave Desert is a grave responsibility. It is a large area, containing thousands of sites of importance to the descendants of these desert peoples, to professional researchers, and to the citizens of the United States, in general. The decisions and actions that are based on these recommendations will have a substantial impact on these resources for years to come.

I have attempted to meet this awesome responsibility by identifying a series of criteria which I feel are particularly relevant to the selection of preservation areas and to the allocation of protection and mitigation measures. Hopefully these may serve, in conjunction with the many alternative criteria offered by researchers elsewhere, as a practical groundwork for the development of a sound conservation plan for the cultural resources of the Western Mojave.

REFERENCES

Bader, J.S. and W.R. Moyle
  1958   Data on water wells and springs in the Morongo Valley and
         vicinity. Ms. on file, United States Geological Survey,
         Long Beach, CA.

Bailey, H.P.
  1966   The climate of Southern California. California Natural
         History Guides 17. University of California Press,
         Berkeley.

Bean, Lowell J. and Charles R. Smith
  1978   Serrano. In Handbook of North American Indians (Vol.
         III), edited by Robert F. Heizer, pp. 570-574. Smith-
         sonian Institution, Washington, D.C.

Belden, L. Burr
  1952   Waterman Mine big producer in silver bullion. "History
         in the Making" Series, San Bernardino Sun-Telegram.
         June 29th, p. 20.

  1954a Dale District long producers of rich gold ore. "History
         in the Making" Series, San Bernardino Sun-Telegram.
         February 21st, p. 22.

  1954b Surveyors have many troubles mapping the desert. "History
         in the Making" Series, San Bernardino Sun-Telegram. July
         25th, p. 31.

Bettinger, Robert L., J.F. O'Connell and R.E. Taylor
  1974   Suggested revisions in archaeological sequences of the
         Great Basin in interior Southern California. Nevada
         Archeological Survey Research Paper 5, Reno.

Blalock, Hubert M.
  1960   Social statistics. McGraw-Hill, New York.

Brooks, George R. (editor)
  1977   The southwest expedition of Jedidiah S. Smith: his
         personal account of the journey to California, 1826-1827.
         A.H. Clark Company, Glendale, CA.

Bryan, Alan P. (editor)
  1978   Early Man in America from a circum-Pacific perspective.
         University of Alberta Printing Service, Edmonton.

Budinger, Fred
  1978   Update on analysis result from the Calico site. Paper
         presented at the Society for California Archaeology Data
         Sharing Meeting, Redlands, CA.

Campbell, Elizabeth W.C.
  1931   An archaeological survey of the Twentynine Palms region.
         Southwest Museum Papers 7, Los Angeles.

Campbell, Elizabeth W.C. and W.H. Campbell
  1935   The Pinto Basin site. Southwest Museum Papers 9, Los
         Angeles.

Campbell, Elizabeth W.C., W.H. Campbell, E. Antevs, C. Amsden, J.
Barbieri and F. Bode
  1937   The archaeology of Pleistocene Lake Mohave. Southwest
         Museum Papers 11, Los Angeles.

Casebier, Dennis G.
  1972   The battle at Camp Cady. Tales of the Mojave Road Pub-
         lishing Company, Norco, CA.

  1975   The Mojave Road. Tales of the Mojave Road Publishing
         Company, Norco, CA.

Chaput, Donald
  1975   Francois X. Aubry, trader, trailmaker and voyageur in the
         Southwest, 1846-1854. A.H. Clark Company, Glendale, CA.

Clewlow, C.W. Jr., Robert F. Heizer, and R. Berger
  1970   An assessment of radiocarbon dates for the Rose Spring
         site (Ca-INY-372), Inyo County, California. Contributions
         of the Archaeological Research Facility 7: 19-27. Univer-
         sity of California, Berkeley.

Cooke, R.U.
  1970   Morphometric analysis of pediments and associated land-
         forms in the western Mojave Desert, California. American
         Journal of Science 269: 26-38.

Cooke, R.U. and A. Warren
  1973   Geomorphology in deserts. University of California Press,
         Berkeley.

Coombs, Gary B.
  1978   The archaeology of the northeast Mojave Desert. Ms. on
         file, Bureau of Land Management, Desert Planning Staff,
         Riverside, CA.

Dibblee, T.W. Jr.
  1958   Tertiary stratigraphic units of the western Mojave Desert,
         California. American Association of Petroleum Geologists
         Bulletin 42(1): 135-144.

  1960a Geologic maps of the Barstow and Hawes quadrangles, San
         Bernardino County, California. United States Survey
         Mineral Investigations Field Studies Maps, MF-233, MF-266.

1960b   Preliminary geologic map of the Shadow Mountains quad-
         rangle, Los Angeles and San Bernardino counties,
         California. United States Geologic Survey Mineral
         Investigations Field Studies Map, MF-227.

1964   Geologic maps of the San Gorgonio Mountains, Lucerne
         Valley, Ord Mountains and Rodman Mountains. United
         States Geologic Survey Miscellaneous Investigations
         Maps, I-426, I-427, I-430.

1967a   Geologic maps of Old Woman Springs, Morongo Valley,
         Joshua Tree and Twentynine Palms. United States
         Geologic Survey Miscellaneous Investigations Maps,
         I-518, I-517, I-516, I-561.

1967b   Areal geology of the western Mojave Desert, California.
         United States Geologic Survey Professional Paper 522.

1970   Geologic map of the Daggett quadrangle, San Bernardino
         County, California. United States Geologic Survey
         Miscellaneous Investigations Map, I-592.

Dixon, Keith A.
  1970   Report of the Calico conference. The Informant 1(10).
         California State University, Long Beach.

Drover, Chris
  1978   Archaeological work in the Cronese Basin. Paper pre-
         sented at the Society of California Archaeology Data
         Sharing Meeting, Redlands, CA.

Edwards, E.I.
  1969   The abandoned state line. The Westerner's Brand Book 13.
         Los Angeles Corral of Westerners, Los Angeles.

Erwin, H.D. and D.L. Gardner
  1940   Notes on the geology of a portion of the Calico Moun-
         tains, San Bernardino County, California. California
         Journal of Mines and Geology 36(3): 293-304.

Euler, Robert C.
  1967   The canyon dwellers. American West 4(2): 22-27, 67-70.

Glennan, William S.
  1976   The Manix Lake lithic industry: Early lithic tradition
         or workshop refuse? Journal of New World Archaeology
         1(7): 43-61.

Hafen, LeRoy and Ann W. Hafen (editors)
  1954   Old Spanish Trail: Santa Fe to Los Angeles. The Far
         West and the Rockies Historical Series: 1820-1875 (Vol.
         I). A.H. Clark Company, Glendale, CA.

Harrington, M.R.
   1957   A Pinto site at Little Lake, California. Southwest
          Museum Papers 17, Los Angeles.

Haynes, C.V.
   1973   The Calico site: Artifacts or geofacts? Science 181:
          305-310.

Hester, Thomas R.
   1973   Chronological ordering of Great Basin prehistory.
          Contributions of the Archaeological Research Facility
          17, University of California, Berkeley.

Hewett, D.F.
   1954a General geology of the Mojave Desert region, California.
          State of California, Division of Mines Bulletin 170(1):
          5-20.

   1954b A fault map of the Mojave Desert region. State of
          California, Division of Mines Bulletin 170(1): 15.

Hidy, Linda
   1971   Harper Dry Lake, a survey and site report. San Ber-
          nardino County Museum Quarterly 19(2).

Hubbs, C., G.S. Bien and H.E. Suess
   1963   La Jolla natural radiocarbon measurements. Radiocarbon
          7: 66-117.

Intertribal Council
   1976   Nuwuvi: Southern Paiute history. University of Utah
          Printing Service, Salt Lake City, UT.

Irwin, H.T.
   1971   Developments in early man studies in western North America,
          1970. Arctic Anthropology 8(2): 42-67.

Jaeger, E.C.
   1957   The North American deserts. Stanford University Press,
          Stanford, CA.

Johnson, Harry R.
   1911   Water resources of Antelope Valley, California. United
          States Geologic Survey Water-Supply Paper 278.

Johnston, F.J.
   1965   The Serrano Indians of Southern California. Malki Museum
          Brochure 2, Banning, California.

Keeling, Patricia J. (editor)
   1976   Reprint of Calico, San Bernardino City and County Directory
          1886. in Once upon a desert: a bicentennial project,
          p. 94. Mojave River Valley Museum Association, Barstow, CA.

King, Chester and Dennis Casebier
  1976   Background to historic and prehistoric resources of the
          east Mojave Desert region. Bureau of Land Management,
          Desert Planning Staff, Riverside, CA.

King, Thomas J.
  1976   Archaeological implications of the paleobotanical record
          from Lucerne Valley area of the Mojave Desert. San Ber-
          nardino County Museum Quarterly 23(4).

Lanning, Edward P.
  1963   Archaeology of the Rose Spring site (INY-372). Univer-
          sity of California Publications in American Archaeology
          and Ethnology 49(3): 237-336.

Leakey, L.S.B., R.D. Simpson and T. Clements
  1968   Archaeological excavations in the Calico Mountains,
          California: Preliminary report. Science 160: 1022-1023.

Mendenhall, Walter C.
  1909   Some desert watering places in southeastern California and
          southwestern Nevada. United States Geologic Survey Water-
          Supply Paper 224.

Mosely, Michael and Gerald A. Smith
  1962   Archaeological investigations of the Mojave River drainage.
          San Bernardino County Museum Quarterly 9(3).

Munz, P.A.
  1974   A flora of Southern California. University of California
          Press, Berkeley.

Munz, P.A. and D.D. Keck
  1949   California plant communities. Aliso 2:87-105.

Myrick, David
  1963   Railroads of Nevada and eastern California (Vol. II).
          Howell-Norton Books, Berkeley, CA.

Norris, Frank and Richard L. Carrico
  1978   A history of land use in the California Desert conservation
          area. Bureau of Land Management, Desert Planning Staff,
          Riverside, CA.

O'Connell, J.F.
  1967   Elko eared/Elko corner-notched projectile points as time
          markers in the Great Basin. University of California
          Archaeological Survey Reports 73: 129-140.

Payne, Nellie
  1976   Coolgardie placer mines. In Once upon a desert: A bicen-
          tennial project, edited by Patricia J. Keeling, p. 108.
          Mojave River Valley Museum Association, Barstow, CA.

Rector, Carol
    1978   Preliminary report: An archaeological data recovery
            program for SBCM-616. Ms. on file, Archaeological
            Research Unit, University of California, Riverside.

Rogers, Malcolm J.
    1939   Early lithic industries of the Lower Basin of the Colorado
            River and adjacent desert areas. San Diego Museum Papers
            3.

San Bernardino County Museum Association
    1972   Review of the Calico excavation, Yermo. San Bernardino
            County Museum Quarterly 19: 3.

Schroeder, Albert H.
    1962   The Hohokam, Sinagua and the Hakayaya. Imperial Valley
            College Museum Society Occasional Paper 3.

Schuiling, Walter C. (editor)
    1972   Pleistocene Man at Calico. San Bernardino County Museum
            Association, Redlands, CA.

Schwartz, Douglas A., Arthur L. Lange and Raymond de Saussure
    1958   Split twig figurines in the Grand Canyon. American
            Antiquity 28: 264-274.

Simpson, Ruth D.
    1958   The Manix Lake archaeological survey. Masterkey 32(1):
            4-10. Southwest Museum, Los Angeles.

    1960   Archaeological survey of the eastern Calico Mountains.
            Masterkey 34: 25-35. Southwest Museum, Los Angeles.

    1961   Coyote Gulch: Archaeological investigations of an early
            lithic locality in the Mohave Desert of San Bernardino
            County. Archaeological Survey Association of Southern
            California 5.

    1964   The archaeological survey of Pleistocene Manix Lake (an
            early lithic horizon). Proceedings of the 35th Inter-
            national Congress of Americanists 35(1): 5-9.

    1965   An archaeological survey of Troy Lake, San Bernardino
            County. San Bernardino County Museum Quarterly 12(3).

    1969   Ice Age archaeology in the Calicos. Pacific Coast
            Archaeological Society Quarterly 5(4): 43-50.

    1978   The Calico Mountains archaeological site. In Early Man
            in North America, edited by Alan Bryan, pp. 218-219.
            Researches International Ltd., Edmonton, Alberta, Canada.

Smith, Gerald A.
   1955   Preliminary report on Schuiling Cave, Newberry, California.
          San Bernardino County Museum Quarterly 3(2).

   1963a Archaeological survey of the Mojave River area and adjacent
          regions. San Bernardino County Museum Association, Redlands,
          CA.

   1963b Split-twig figurines from San Bernardino County, California.
          Masterkey 37: 86-90. Southwest Museum, Los Angeles.

Smith, Gerald A., Charles LaMonk, T.E. Forman, Shirley Hill and
Charles Howe
   1961   Indian picture writing of San Bernardino and Riverside
          counties. San Bernardino County Museum Quarterly 8(3).

Smith, Gerald A., W. Schuiling, L. Martin, R. Sayles and P. Jillson
   1957   Newberry Cave, California. San Bernardino County Museum
          Quarterly 4(3).

Smith, Gerald A., and W.G. Turner
   1977   Indian rock art of Southern California. San Bernardino
          County Museum Association, Redlands, CA.

Susia, Margaret L.
   1964   Tule Springs archaeological surface survey. Nevada State
          Museum Anthropological Papers 12.

Thomas, David H. and Robert L. Bettinger
   1976   Prehistoric piñon ecotone settlements of the Upper Reese
          River Valley, central Nevada. Anthropological Papers of
          the American Museum of Natural History 3(5).

Thompson, David G.
   1921   Routes to desert watering places in the Mojave Desert
          region, California. United States Geologic Survey Water-
          Supply Paper 490-B.

Turner, Wilson G.
   1978   Recording petroglyphs, a 1977 preliminary report on the
          Black Canyon project of the Mojave Desert. San Bernardino
          County Museum Quarterly 24(3).

Turner, Wilson G., E. Popiano and Robert Reynolds
   1971   Three essays on petroglyphology. San Bernardino County
          Museum Quarterly 19(1).

Vasek, F.C. and M.G. Barbour
   1977   Mojave Desert scrub vegetation. In Terrestrial vegetation
          of California, edited by M.G. Barbour and Fred Major, pp.
          835-868. John Wiley and Sons,

Vasek, F.C. and R.F. Thorne
   1977   Transmontane coniferous vegetation. In _Terrestrial Vegetation of California_, edited by M.G. Barbour and Major, pp. 797-834. John Wiley and Sons.

Vita-Finzi, C. and E. Higgs
   1971   Prehistoric economy in the Mount Carmel area of Palestine: site catchment analysis. _Proceedings of the Prehistoric Society_ 36: 1-37.

Walker, H.M. and J. Lev
   1953   _Statistical inference_. Holt, Rinehart and Winston, New York.

Wallace, William J.
   1962   Prehistoric cultural development in the Southern California deserts. _American Antiquity_ 28: 172-180.

   1978   Post Pleistocene archaeology, 9000 to 2000 B.C. In _Handbook of North American Indians_ (Vol. VIII), edited by Robert F. Heizer, pp. 25-36. Smithsonian Institution, Washington, D.C.

Warren, Claude N.
   1967   The San Dieguito complex: A review and hypothesis. _American Antiquity_ 32(2): 168-185.

Warren, Claude N. and Robert H. Crabtree
   n.d.   The prehistory of the southwestern Great Basin. In _Handbook of North American Indians_, edited by William Sturtevant. Smithsonian Institution, Washington, D.C., in press.

Warren, Claude N. and Anthony J. Ranere
   1968   Outside Danger Cave: A view of early man in the Great Basin. _Contributions in Anthropology_ 1(4): 6-18. Eastern New Mexico University, Clovis, NM.

Warren, Claude N. and D.L. True
   1961   The San Dieguito complex and its place in California prehistory. _Archaeological Survey Annual Report 1960-1961_, 246-338. University of California, Los Angeles.

Warren, Elizabeth von Till
   1974   _Armijo's trace revisited: A new interpretation of the impact of the Antonio Armijo route of 1829-1830 on the development of the Old Spanish Trail_. Unpublished M.A. thesis, University of Nevada, Las Vegas.

Warren, Elizabeth von Till and Ralph T. Roske
   1978   Cultural resources of the California Desert 1776-1880: Historic trails and wagon roads. Ms. on file, Bureau of Land Management, Desert Planning Staff, Riverside, CA.

Weinberg, George H. and John A. Schumaker
   1962   Statistics: An intuitive approach. Brooks/Cole Publishing
          Company, Belmont, CA.

Zeitelhack, June and Jan Zeitelhack La Barge
   1976   Operations of the Pacific Coast Borax Company 1883-1907.
          In Once upon a desert: A bicentennial project, edited
          by Patricia J. Keeling, pp. 96-104. Mojave River Valley
          Museum Association, Barstow, CA.

APPENDIX I

BLM SITE CLASSIFICATION SYSTEM

A. ARCHAEOLOGICAL SITE TYPES. An <u>archaeological site</u> is defined as a locus of prehistoric activities which can be delineated specifically by the cultural remains present and can be separated by distance and/or observable geomorphic features from other loci of prehistoric activities (Historic sites are covered elsewhere). The cultural materials that constitute a site are basically artifacts and/or cultural features. <u>Artifacts</u> are objects manufactured or modified by man, such as projectile points, manos, metates, bone awls, etc. <u>Cultural features</u> are specific clusters of artifacts and/or other material used or assembled by man that exhibit structural association and that consist of nonrecoverable or composite matrices. Examples of cultural features are burials, roasting pits, bedrock mortars, pictographs, etc. The smallest spatial unit with which the archaeologist deals is the site. Therefore, a single artifact by itself, found with no other cultural material, becomes an archaeological site. Similarly, an isolated cultural feature (e.g., roasting pit) becomes an archaeological site. Most archaeological sites are made up of a cluster of artifacts or a cluster of artifacts with an associated cultural feature(s). This is illustrated as follows:

SITE

ARTIFACT ⟶ FEATURE

For planning purposes and to facilitate discussion of prehistoric behavior within the study area, 17 site types and 8 sub-types have been designated. Although initially developed to assist other Bureau specialists and Bureau management in understanding the variety of aboriginal activities manifested in the archaeological record, the archaeological site types used here have also turned out to be useful to the archaeologist working with the available data. They provide the archaeologist with a general category in which to place each site presently in the existing record. Obviously not all the sites will fit neatly into one or another of the site types but it does provide a means to begin dealing with the diversity in the archaeological record.

The site type given each archaeological site is determined by the information provided on the site record sheet. The existing site record sheets are limited in the amount of information they can provide. The site type given is the most accurate judgement that can be made based on the information available. The site types are flexible enough so that if additional information becomes available then the site type(s) can be changed if change is warranted.

Each site type has been given a descriptive name in order to make recognition easier and, on an extremely generalized level, to function as an activity indicator. The 17 archaeological site types and 8 sub-types are described as follows:

01 <u>Village</u> - This site type represents long-term or seasonal activity, usually identified as a village or base camp. A village would be identified archaeologically by primary and secondary tools (that is, tools used in the manufacture of other tools) and a variety of other artifacts, as well as floral and faunal remains which represented subsistence activities. Such a site would be characterized by extensive scatters and quantities of debris such as potsherds, fire-affected rock, whole and broken flaked stone tools, chipping waste, charred bone, milling tools, house structures, hearths, rock rings, and sometimes rock art or burials and cremations. A well developed midden is usually a component of this site type.

02 <u>Temporary Camp</u> - Temporary camps are sites that were occupied for a short length of time (e.g., one day to one month) by a few people (from an individual to several families). These sites can be identified archaeologically by scattered artifacts, tool manufacturing debris, fire-affected rocks and possibly features. They differ from the first site type by size and frequency of cultural remnants. This type is somewhat a catch-all category. It includes sites that reflect a range of artifacts and/or cultural features that in combination do not allow the site to be typed in another category (e.g., pottery with flakes). The inferred function of the site is limited camping (i.e., limited subsistence and maintenance activities). However, an open site with any combination of flaked stone artifacts, ground stone, fire-affected rocks, and/or ceramics could fit in this site type.

03 <u>Utilized Shelter or Cave</u> - This site type represents archaeological sites found exclusively in rockshelters caves or under rock overhangs. If only rock art is present then the site is typed as 12 or 13. Three sub-types have been identified. These are as follows:

03a <u>Occupation Rockshelter</u> - This sub-type represents temporary or seasonal occupation locations containing cultural debris similar to that described for village locations (01) or temporary camps (02).

03b <u>Transient Rockshelter</u> - Rockshelter or overhang indicative of extremely limited use. The inferred use is that of overnight camping enroute to other locations. These sites are usually along an aboriginal trail or route of travel. Cultural remains may consist only of an isolated tool or a few flakes and possibly some fire-affected rocks. Absent from this type is a developed midden.

03c <u>Storage Rock Shelter</u> - Rockshelter or overhang, usually small in size, containing only basketry, pottery, or other cultural remains indicative of storage activities. This would include tool or food caches.

04 <u>Milling Station</u> - This site type is a manifestation of procurement and/or processing of hard (e.g., chia) and/or soft (e.g., acorn) seeds and other food items. Associated artifacts may include manos, metates, mortars or pestles. Bedrock mortars or bedrock metates (e.g., grinding slicks or rubs) may be present. This site type may consist of an isolated metate or a single bedrock metate or any combination of

artifacts or features indicative of milling activities. Associated
with this site type may be an occasional flake or flaked stone tool.

05 <u>Lithic Scatter</u> - These sites are characterized exclusively by the
presence of flaked stone tools, chipping waste, cores, retouched and
utilized flakes, and/or flake material such as chalcedony, chert,
jasper, opal, rhyolite, or obsidian. Other cultural material is
absent. Since this general site type often constitutes a major
percentage of the archaeological site inventory, five sub-types are
used here to allow a closer assessment of this type's variability.

From the existing site record sheets, only the variables of 1) area
and 2) <u>density or quantity</u> of flaked stone material present can be
determined with any regularity. Giving two characteristics to each of
the major variables, four combinations are possible.

The characteristics for area are simply 1) large, and 2) small.
<u>Large</u> is considered to be greater than 50 square meters. <u>Small</u> is
considered to be less than 50 square meters.

For density of quantity, the characteristics are 1) high, and 2) low.
The determination of the characteristics is dependent on key terms
used on the site record sheet or on the number of artifacts observed.

A <u>high density</u> is determined if terms such as "dense," "heavy,"
"thick," "numerous," "a wide variety," etc., are used in reference to
quantity of flakes and/or flaked stone tools present. If only the
number or a listing of flakes and/or flaked stone tools observed is
given then a rough assessment of artifacts per ten square meters is
made. Generally, an estimate of an average of more than 30 flakes
and/or flaked stone tools per ten square meters is considered high.

A <u>low density</u> is determined if terms such as "thin," "few," "light,"
"small number," etc., are used in reference to quantity of flakes
and/or flaked stone tools present. If only the number or a listing
of flakes and/or flaked stone tools observed is given then a rough
assessment of artifacts per ten square meters is made. Generally,
an estimate of an average of less than 30 flakes and/or flaked stone
tools per ten squre meters is considered low.

The four combinations of area and density are shown as follows:

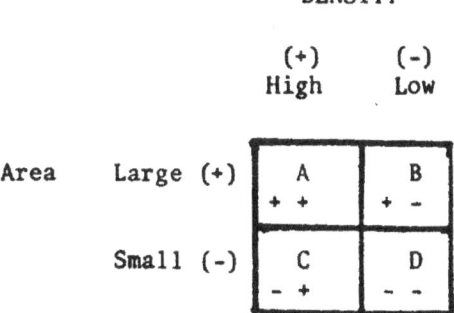

DENSITY

		(+) High	(-) Low
Area	Large (+)	A + +	B + -
	Small (-)	C - +	D - -

The fifth sub-type, Chipping Circle, is a distinct archaeological feature which when occurring without other flaked stone material or flaked stone tools is recorded as an archaeological site.

The five sub-types of Lithic Scatters are briefly described as follows:

05a **Large, Dense Lithic Scatter** - A locus consisting of a high density of flakes and/or flaked stone tools over a large area (i.e., high density and large area).

05b **Large, Light Lithic Scatter** - A locus consisting of a low density of flakes and/or flaked stone tools over a large area (i.e., low density and large area).

05c **Small, Dense Lithic Scatter** A locus consisting of a high density of flakes and/or flaked stone tools over a small area (i.e., high density and small area).

05d **Small, Light Lithic Scatter** - A locus consisting of a low density of flakes and/or flaked stone tools over a small area (i.e., low density and small area).

05e **Chipping Circle** A loci consisting simply of a core with related flakes immediately around it. Occasionally, flakes from the core evidence possible utilization. Hammerstone(s) may on occasion be found in association. A "chipping circle" is usually only one or two meters in diameter. A cluster of chipping circles (i.e., two or more) may be considered a single site if they are less than 20 meters apart and more than 100 meters from another site. Occasionally, an isolated flake or flakedstone tool may be found in the vicinity of a chipping circle. If a chipping circle is associated with other flakes and/or flaked stone tools, or if it is part of a larger site, then another site type or sub-type is utilized.

06 **Quarry** - A quarry site is a location where lithic material has been extracted from a larger mass (usually crypto-crystalline), such as a seam, vein or outcrop, for the purpose of tool manufacture. Such sites are characterized by an abundance of flakes, cores, occasional hammerstones, preforms, blanks or rejects.

07 **Pottery Scatter** - This type of site is represented by surface scatters of pottery (ceramic) sherds or broken vessels. No other artifacts or features are present.

08 **Cemetery** - Prehistoric locations for human internment comprise this site type. Surface indications may include cairns, exposed bone, mounding or markers. This site type ranges from isolated burials in shallow holes to extensive cemeteries.

09 **Cremation Locus** - A special type of internment is the cremation. Charred human bone fragments may occasionally be found in small cavities in the rock, in dune areas, in utilized shelters or caves, or as part of camps or villages.

10 Intaglio - These are large figures produced on desert pavement surfaces
   in the form of animal, human, and geometric designs. Their distribution
   is usually limited to areas along the lower Colorado River or Yuha Desert
   but isolated occurrences in other areas have been noted.

11 Rock Alignment - Prehistoric alignments of cobbles and boulders occur in
   the California Desert. Such alignments vary in size and complexity
   ranging from simple lines to complex abstract or geometric designs.

12 Petroglyph Site - Petroglyphs represent pecked or incised figures or
   designs on boulders, rock outcrops or shelter walls.

13 Pictograph Site - Pictographs are painted figures or designs which occur
   most frequently on the walls of sheltered caves, boulders or outcrops.
   The most frequent colors are red, black and white although other colors
   such as orange, brown, yellow and green can occur.

        Note: If both petroglyphs and pictographs are present then
               the dominate rock art form (i.e., greatest number of
               elements) dictates the site type to be given (e.g.,
               petroglyph site with pictographs or pictograph site
               with petroglyphs.) The lesser rock art form (i.e.,
               smallest number of elements) is recorded as a cultural
               feature.

14 Trail - Trails are marked routes of travel between permanent villages,
   temporary camps, and resource procurement areas. Where they survive,
   trails usually are faint linear impressions or clearings in the desert
   pavement or slight "shelves" along hillsides and canyon slopes. Potsherds
   and other artifacts may occur along trails, as might rock cairns or trail
   shrines. However, the trail is an entity in itself--a route of travel
   interlinking the various activity areas and sites of the aboriginal
   populations.

15 Roasting Pit - This site type encompasses the range of rock features
   which includes earth ovens, roasting pits and clusters of fire affected
   rock. This category is used when there is an absence of other cultural
   remains.

16 Isolated Find - An occurence of a single artifact or cultural features
   that does not conform to other site types are documented with this
   category. This includes isolated flaked stone tools, cores, manos, and
   other artifacts not covered by other site types (e.g., an isolated
   metate is included in 04). Cultural features included in this site
   type are single rock rings or single sleeping circles with no associated
   artifacts or other cultural features.

17 Cairn - Mounding of cobbles and/or boulders are found in the California
   Desert. These are referred to as rock cairns. Sometimes cairns mark
   trails, shrines, or burials. Cairns can appear singularly or in clusters.

B. HISTORICAL SITE TYPES. For purposes of this section, historic sites are defined as loci of past activity or activities of Hispanic and Euro-American populations. It includes sites documented in the historic record (i.e., diaries, historic accounts, andother historic documents) and sites for which no written record or reference can be found. The historic period in the study area dates back to 1776. At the other end, a site is normally considered "historic" if it is 40 years or older. However, more recent sites that have maintained historical integrity (e.g., homesteads) or are associated with a significant event or activity (e.g., WW II training camps) may also be included.

More than two dozen historical site types have been identified in localized areas within the California desert. These site types can be placed into five cultural categories which are indicative of general activities. These cultural categories or general activities are 1) Exploration, 2) Settlement 3) Military, 4) Mining, and 5) Transportation.

1. Exploration involves historical sites associated with early expeditions, explorations, immigrations, and government surveys. Sites associated with this category are simply campsites and routes of travel.

2. Settlement includes those sites indicative of living activities and maintenance activities associated with settlement. Sites within this category include town, hamlet, mining camp, dug out, homestead, farm, ranch, school, cemetery, well, trash dump, and other structures associated with settlement.

3. Military encompasses remnants of past military activities. Sites of this category are fort, camp, outpost, redoubt, and World War II training camp.

4. Mining is a category to cover activities specifically related to the extraction and processing of locatable, salable and/or hardrock minerals. Sites included in this category are mine, shaft, addit, tunnel, mill, arrastre, and mining works.

5. Transportation deals with historical sites that were involved with public conveyance of passengers and/or goods, especially for a commercial enterprise, and sites directly related to this activity. Sites within this category are pack trail, wagon road, stage route, early automobile road, railroad, railroad station and water stopovers.

The various site types are briefly described as follows:

01 Town - A compactly settled area usually larger than a hamlet.

02 Hamlet - A small settlement.

03 Mining Camp - A settlement associated specifically with mining activities. This is also indicative of much more transient use than either 01 or 02.

04 Homestead - A tract of land acquired from U.S. public lands
    by filing a record and living on and cultivating the tract.

05 Farm - A plot of land devoted to the raising of crops.

06 Ranch - A plot of land devoted to the raising of beef cattle and/
    or other livestock.

07 Railroad Station - The building, remains, and/or regularly
    scheduled stopping place of the train for the purpose of
    loading and unloading passengers and freight.

08 Post Office - A building and/or site once officially designated
    as a local branch of the U.S. Post Office.

09 School - A building used for educational instruction.

10 Structure - Something that is constructed (e.g., building) of
    rock, adobe, wood, or a combination of these materials or other
    material.

11 Fort - An official U.S. military designation for a permanent army
    post that is occupied continuously by troops.

12 Camp (1800's) - The lowest official U.S. military designation
    for an army post that is usually small but has a permanent
    detachment of men assigned to it.

13 Camp (WW II) - An official military post consisting mostly of
    tent structures and established as a base of operation for World
    War II training manuevers.

14 Outpost - An unofficial military designation used in the 1860's
    to identify a temporary post to which a small detachment of men
    (usually a non-commissioned officer and 3-10 enlisted men) from
    a regional camp were temporarily assigned.

15 Redoubt - A small, usually temporary, enclosed defensive work.

16 Mine - A pit or excavation in the earth from which mineral
    substances are taken.

17 Shaft - A vertical or inclined opening of uniform and limited cross
    section made for finding or mining ore.

18 Addit - A horizontal opening of uniform and limited cross section
    made for finding or mining ore.

19 Tunnel - A horizontal passageway through a ridge, hill or mountain
    and associated with mining activities.

20 Arrastre - A devise built to grind gold-bearing quartz. The early
    types consisted of a low stone and dirt wall built around a large
    and fairly level stone, hard pan or flat rock-lined floor.

A long horizontal beam was pivoted on a vertical post in the arrastre's center. One end of the beam was harnessed to a burro or mule to provide necessary power by walking in a circle outside the low arrastre wall. A heavy chain was fastened to the beam about midway, and the free end of the chain linked to a ring bolt wedged in a heavy drag stone(s).

21 Ore Mill - A site where crushing machinery, usually steam engine powered, was used to pulverize ore-bearing rock to facilitate the extraction of gold and/or other metals. Five- and ten-stamp mills were most common.

22 Mining Works An area where mining and/or processing works (e.g., flumes, chutes, sorters, etc.) are present.

23 Dug Out - A shelter dug in a hillside or dug in the ground and roofed with sod or earth.

24 Railroad - The remains of a permanent road having a line of rails fixed to ties and laid on a roadbed or berm and providing tracks for railroad cars.

25 Automobile Road (Early) - Road used for early automobile travel (e.g., Model-T, etc.).

26 Wagon Road - Route habitually used by wagons pulled by draft animals.

27 Stage Route - Trail utilized regularly by the stagecoach companies for handling passengers and mail.

28 Pack Trail - Historic foot and pack animal (horse and mule) route of travel that was not used by wagons.

29 Exploration Route - Routes taken by early expeditions, explorers, travelers, and survey parties. Also included are routes used for domestic livestock drives.

30 Cemetery - A place with historic human internments associated with Euro-American activities (i.e., a historic burial ground).

31 Trash Dump - A place where refuse or other discarded materials are accumulated or dumped.

32 Well - A deep hole or shaft sunk into the earth to tap an underground supply of water.

33 Railroad Water Stop - A place along a railroad right-of-way where trains periodically stopped to take on water.

34 Isolated Find Singular occurance of a historic artifact such as the following:

> Bottle
> Stirrup
> Horseshoe
>
> Road grader

CALIFORNIA DESERT PROGRAM
ARCHAEOLOGICAL SAMPLE UNIT RECORD

1. Planning Unit_____ 2. Sample Unit #_____ 3. Date_____

4. Twp._____ Range_____ Section_____ 5. Map_____

6. General Location:

7. Vegetation:

8. Fauna:

9. Geology/Geomorphology:

10. Hydrology:

11. Weather Conditions:

12. Sites Recorded:

13. Duration of Survey:

14. Survey Crew:

Recorder:_____

15. <u>General Interpretations & Comments</u> (Attach additional pages as necessary):

16. <u>Sketch Map of Sample Unit</u>   Indicate: a) Dimensions of sample unit;
     b) Pertinent or prominant land forms; c) Survey pattern, including
     approximate area covered and portion of unit covered by individual
     crew members; d) Location of sites recorded.

BLM CALIFORNIA
HISTORIC SITE SURVEY FORM

County _____
District _____
Planning Unit _____
Sample Unit _____
Photos _____
Date _____
Recorder _____

1. Site Number _____ 2. Site Name _____
3. Other (numbers/names) _____
4. Location: Twn ____, Rng ____, ____of
____, of Sec ____, Quad _____, Elev _____
Reference Points: _____
_____

UTM Grid Loc: Zone _____ North _____ East _____

5. Ownership: BLM __, Other Federal __, State __, Private __, Unk __

6. National Register Status: Candidate __, Potential __, Determined
not Elgible __, No Determination __,

7. Disturbance: Animal __, Burning __, Vandalism __, ORV __,
Other __, Explain_____
_____

8. Present Condition: Good __, Fair __, Poor __, Explain _____
_____

9. Activity: Mining __, Railroad __, Military __, Homesteading __,
Exploration/Traveling __, Settlement __, Ranching __,
Other __, Explain _____

10. Site Type: Town __, Camp __, Homestead __, Road __, Trail __,
Mine __, Railroad __, Graveyard __, Trashdump __,
Military __, Other _____

11. Features: Structure __, Dugout __, Fire Hearth __, Cairn __,
Rock Alignment __, Trashdump __, Irrigation __,
Trail __, Road __, Corral __, Burial __, Well __,
Spring __, R&R Grade (berm) __, Tram (road/way) __,
Tailings __, Other __, Explain _____
_____

12. Artifacts: Wood (size,type) __, Glass (color) __, Metal (type) _
Bone (species) __, Ceramic (color) __, Adobe (con-
dition) __, Nails (size,type) __, Cans (size,type) _
Ordnance __, Other___, Explain _____
_____

13. Temporal Period: Circa _____, Era _____

(continue on reverse side,
refer by number)

BLM CALIFORNIA

ARCHAEOLOGICAL SITE SURVEY RECORD
(Continuation Sheet)

[8] Site # _____   [9] Other # _____
[10] Site Name _____

[1] County	_____
[2] District	_____
[3] Planning Unit	_____
[4] Sample Unit	_____
[5] Photos	_____
[6] Date	_____
[7] Recorder	_____

BLM CALIFORNIA

ARCHAEOLOGICAL SITE SURVEY RECORD

| [1] County |
| [2] District |
| [3] Planning Unit |
| [4] Sample Unit |
| [5] Photos |
| [6] Date |
| [7] Recorder |

[8] Site # _____ [9] Other # _____

[10] Site Name _____

[11] Cadastral Location: Twn ____ Rng ____ ____ of ____ of Sec ____

[12] Quadrangle _____ [13] Elevation _____

[14] UTM Grid Loc. Zone _____ Northing _____ Easting _____

[15] Reference Points: _____

_____

[16] OWNER

BLM	OTHER FED.	STATE	PRIVATE	UNKNOWN

[17] NAT'L REGISTER

(A) STATUS					(B) TYPE		
LISTED	CANDIDATE	POTENTIAL	NOT ELG.	NO DET.	DISTRICT	SITE	OTHER

[18] DISTURB

DEVELOPMENT	ANIMAL	VANDALISM	ORV	OTHER

[19] CNDT

GOOD	FAIR	POOR

[20] COMMENTS

[21] SITE TYPES

VILLAGE	TEMPORARY CAMP	SHELTER/CAVE	MILLING STA.	LITHIC SCATTER	QUARRY SITE	POTTERY LOCUS	CEMETERY	CREMATION LOCUS	INTAGLIO	ROCK ALIGNMENT	PETROGLYPH	PICTOGRAPH	TRAIL	ROASTING PIT	ISOLATED FIND	CAIRN	HISTORIC	OTHER

[22] AREA

0-10 Sq. M.	11-50	51-250	251-1000	1001-5000	over 5000

[23] DEPTH

SURFACE	1-20 Cm.	21-100	over 100	UNKNOWN

[24] General Site Description:

[25] FEATURES

STRUCTURAL DEP.	ROCK RING	ROCK STRUCTURE	CAIRN /SHRINE	ROASTING PIT/FAR	HEARTH	PETROGLYPHS	PICTOGRAPHS	BEDROCK MORTAR	GRINDING SLICK	OTHER

[26] ARTIFACTS

PROJECTILE POINT	FLAKED STONE TOOL	CORE-DETRITUS	MILLING TOOL	OTHER GROUND STONE	CERAMIC	BONE	PERISHABLE	ORNAMENT	HISTORIC	OTHER

[27] ECO.

FIRE AFFECTED ROCK	FAUNA	FLORA	OTHER

[28] MAT.

CRYPTOCRYSTALLINE	OBSIDIAN	FELSITE	OTHER

[29] Describe:

[30] VEGETATION

BARREN	SALTBUSH	CREOSOTE	JOSHUA/CREOSOTE	JOSHUA/YUCCA	YUCCA/CACTUS	BLACKBRUSH	SAGEBRUSH	PINYON/JUNIPER	CONIFER	SHADSCALE	CHAPARRAL	OAK WOODLAND	MESQUITE	RIPARIAN	WASH	GRASSLAND	OTHER

[31] COVERAGE

CONTINUOUS (over75%)	INTERRUPTED (50-75%)	PARK-LIKE (25-50%)	RARE (6-25%)	BARELY PRESENT (1-5%)	ABSENT (0-1%)

[32] WATER

INTERMITTENT STREAM	PERMANENT STREAM	SPRING	PLAYA	OTHER

[33] Describe

[34] LANDFORM

MOUNTAIN	HILL	TERRACE	RIDGE	ALLUVIAL FAN	CANYON	ARROYO	SAND DUNE	DESERT PAVEMENT	BADLANDS	PLAYA	OTHER

[35] BEDROCK

EXTRUSIVE IG.	INTRUSIVE IG.	METAMORPHIC	SEDIMENTARY	QUATERNARY ALLUV.	OTHER

[36] TEXTURE

SAND	LOAM	SILT	CLAY	OTHER

[37] SOILS

MIDDEN	ALLUVIAL	COLLUVIAL	EOLIAN	BEDROCK	OTHER

[38] Describe

[39] SLOPE

POINT OF INFLEX	LOWER 1/3	MID 1/3	UPPER 1/3	0-5°	6-15°	16-30°	31-60°	over 60°

[40] ASPECT

NORTH	NORTH/EAST	EAST	SOUTH/EAST	SOUTH	SOUTH/WEST	WEST	NORTH/WEST

[41] EROSION

DEFLATION	RILLING	GULLYING	SHEET/WASH	ROCK/DEBRIS	SLUMPING	OTHER

[42] DRAIN.

CONVERGING	DIVERGING	BRAIDED	OTHER

[43] Remarks

ARCHAEOLOGICAL PHOTOGRAPHIC RECORD

YEAR	FILM TYPE	CAMERA & LENS TYPE	FILM SPEED	DAY	TUNG	PAGE NO.

Mo.	Day	Time	E+D Frame	SUBJECT	SITE NO.	Cat. No.
			1		05 -	
			2		05 -	
			3		05 -	
			4		05 -	
			5		05 -	
			6		05 -	
			7		05 -	
			8		05 -	
			9		05 -	
			10		05 -	
			11		05 -	
			12		05 -	
			13		05 -	
			14		05 -	
			15		05 -	
			16		05 -	
			17		05 -	
			18		05 -	
			19		05 -	
			20		05 -	
			21		05 -	
			22		05 -	
			23		05 -	
			24		05 -